The
VIETNAMESE
Market
COOKBOOK

SPICY | SOUR | SWEET

by Van Tran and Anh Vu

Photography by Yuki Sugiura

RUNNING PRESS
PHILADELPHIA · LONDON

First published in Great Britain in 2013 by Square Peg
Random House, 20 Vauxhall Bridge Road, London SW1V 2SA
www.vintage-books.co.uk

Copyright © 2014 by Van Tran and Anh Vu

Published by Running Press,
A Member of the Perseus Books Group

Printed in China

ISBN 978-0-7624-5384-9
Library of Congress Control Number: 2013951599
E-book ISBN 978-0-7624- 5529-4

9 8 7 6 5 4 3 2 1
Digit on the right indicates the number of this printing

Cover and interior design by Jason Kayser
Food styling by Valerie Berry
Prop styling by Cynthia lnions
Typography: Calluna and Whitney

To reflect the mood of Vietnam—the slow pace, the
craftsmanship, and the resourcefulness—most of the photographs in this book were shot on conventional negative film.

Running Press Book Publishers
2300 Chestnut Street
Philadelphia, PA 19103-4371

Visit us on the web!
www.offthemenublog.com

To our mothers, for beginning
To our Banhmily, for continuing

Contents

INTRODUCTION

We were born in Vietnam, a land of bustlingly vibrant food markets. They come to life at dawn, with the clattering of footsteps, straw baskets full of local vegetables and seasonal herbs, wheelbarrows weighted down with meat, sacks of freshly baked baguettes, buckets with fish swimming inside, coops with chickens, bamboo presses with fresh tofu, hampers full of specialty mushrooms and spices, and food stalls everywhere. The markets are in the back alleys of Hanoi, in the shadow of high-rises in Saigon, in the misty valleys of Sapa, and on floating boats in the red waters of the Mekong Delta. Cooking, commerce, and community make up the rhythm of daily life in Vietnam, and the starting point is a morning visit to the market. . . .

Five Fundamental Flavors

In Vietnamese cuisine, the ideal food balances the five flavors of sweet, sour, spicy, bitter, and salty. Accordingly, we have arranged the recipes in this book into five chapters, each devoted to one of the five flavors, to help you intuitively understand the principles of Vietnamese cooking. Try to imagine the taste of the dish on the tip of your tongue and then let your palate guide you as you cook.

Each chapter is then divided into three sections. In Vietnam we distinguish between three kinds of eating: *an com, an qua*, and *an choi. An* means "to eat," but it prefixes many other Vietnamese words, which just goes to show how food is at the heart of our culture.

Everyday cooking we call *An Com*, which literally means "to eat rice." This is the classic Vietnamese staple, eaten twice daily. In family meals rice forms the foundation of a holy trinity of first, a savory meat or fish; secondly, a vegetable stir-fry; and last, an accompanying soup. But today, with our busy lifestyles, we are unlikely to cook all these elements for a simple midweek dinner. Instead, you can mix and match these recipes to make healthy everyday meals.

Festive cooking we call *An Qua. Qua* means "a gift." Often in Vietnam, the gift is the amazing combination of flavors in a bowl of noodle soup. Festive cooking can be elaborate, so it's for weekends and celebrations, or simply for when you want to treat yourself.

Social cooking is *An Choi. Choi* means "play." This is eating for enjoyment's sake, such as a snack from a specialist one-dish street-food vendor. Here we have included recipes for starters, snacks, drinks, and sweet treats. These recipes are perfect for shared plates, party canapés, or whenever you fancy bold flavors.

Cooking the Vietnamese Way

An important part of cooking Vietnamese food is learning to develop your own palate: by touching the ingredients, smelling the marinated food, tasting the cooked food, and having the confidence to adjust as you see fit. Every family in Vietnam has a distinct way of cooking, a personal take on what is otherwise a rather orthodox repertoire of dishes. For instance, caramelized braised pork in the north is saltier and saucier than its southern counterpart, which is sweeter and uses coconut milk.

With Vietnam's long history as a sea-facing country with foreign settlers, it's no surprise that our food is a fusion of international influences. Take two of the world's greatest culinary traditions, French and Chinese, throw in a basketful of tropical flavors and fresh herbs, add a dash of Japanese sensitivity, and you have the basis of many of the recipes in Vietnam. Consequently, Vietnamese cooking lends itself to adaptation.

Food markets are ubiquitous in Vietnam. It's here that trading and farming, metropolitan and village life come together as growers and consumers interact. Vietnamese cooking is based on market-fresh ingredients. We look for whatever is in season, harvested that day. We understand that while farm-fresh vegetables might not be perfectly uniform and identically packaged, they will be bursting with flavor. Our cooking is naturally intuitive and versatile. We cook by what the season brings and the market offers, not by the vagaries of celebrity chefs!

Our Story

Van Tran

Anh and I were born eleven months apart in the same city, Hanoi. The capital was previously known as Ke Cho, which translates as "marketplace."

My earliest memory is of holding my mother's hand down a street lined with purple blossoming bang lang trees on our way to the local market. The daily trip to the market was a ritual: at the entrance fruit stands were overflowing with lychees and papayas; further on, butchers' stalls each specialized in one type of meat. My mother would select a cut of meat and plan the day's menu around it. She would visit the dry goods stalls for spices by weight and noodles in all shapes and sizes. To complete the meal she would pick a vegetable for soup, another for a stir-fry, and a handful of fresh herbs. These daily trips to the market gave us joy at the table. They instilled in me not only a love of food but also an appreciation of how it brings people together and spreads warmth.

Markets were so ingrained in our consciousness, that when Anh and I visited Broadway Market in London's East End a year after we moved to the UK, we instantly recognized a missing piece of our lives. There's Matthew, who raises his cows and pigs on organic land in Suffolk. Then there's Jony, who sells sourdough bread so tasty we have midweek cravings. And there's Tamami, who single-handedly bakes wholesome cakes in her small kitchen oven while her children sleep. We identified with these people, their market-fresh way of eating and their sense of community. Echoing our childhood rituals, Saturday morning visits to Broadway Market became a routine. Then, as the kitchen gods would have it, we became stallholders at Broadway Market—Banhmi11 was born in the summer of 2009. We started out with recipes passed down from Anh's mother, who used to have a banh mi stall in Hanoi. For the first year, we made pâté, roast pork, and pickles in our tiny home kitchen and brought everything to the stall on the back of our bicycles. What followed is what happens after love at first bite.

SWEETNESS
&
HAPPINESS

Chapter 1

Sweetness is perhaps the most obviously pleasing of the five flavors. Its familiarity stretches back to childhood treats, like the colorful birthday cakes that marked our annual milestones.

By sweetness we don't just mean the puddings and treats that would classify as a "sweet" on a Western menu. We mean the subtle notes that underpin certain dishes, be they savory or sweet. This chapter includes some obviously sweet ingredients like seductive soft fruits. But it also includes more unlikely candidates: vegetables such as pumpkin and squash, which add a sweet note to soup within minutes; and meat and seafood, which, when cooked the right way, release a deep and succulent sweetness.

The savory recipes in this chapter all have sweet qualities—for example, the pork belly, which is steeped in caramelized sugar and then slowly simmered to release a wonderfully honeyed flavor. In this chapter we include a classic Vietnamese noodle soup called pho. For us, pho is all about sweetness, despite being a main course. In the same way Western soups use stock, pho is based on a broth made from slowly boiled bones. This slow-cooked broth releases a delightful sweetness which is intrinsic to the dish.

Anh and I still believe that truly authentic pho noodle soup is only found in the Old Quarter of Hanoi. The Hanoian palate prefers a gentle sweetness, not the saccharine, MSG-laden offerings of ersatz versions. Hanoi's pho is simple: a clear stock, tender meat, a fine sprinkling of fresh herbs, a couple of slices of fresh chile, a wedge of lime, and no cluttering with bean sprouts.

The soul of this pho is the broth: the fragrance is irresistible, with hints of cinnamon, cardamom, star anise, coriander seeds, and ginger. The sweetness of pho is deep: it doesn't hit the tip of your tongue, but leaves a satisfying kick at the back of your throat.

The first time I had pho in Vietnam as a grown-up was on my first return visit after moving away, and it was then that I understood why my mother had always gone to the effort of making this dish during the years we lived outside Vietnam.

We sat on plastic stools in the heat of Hanoi in July and watched as steaming ladles of broth were poured into large white bowls that gleamed in the early morning sun. Here in Vietnam, street food is simply home cooking that has sprawled out onto the street. People open up their shopfront living rooms, put out more chairs and tables on the pavement, and serve from a stall set up by the entrance.

As we sipped the pho, my mother commented on how soft the fresh, hand-made noodles were. I had never seen her so content, so at home. For the first time, I saw her as a friend, as a person with her own life story, secrets, and dreams. And for the first time I understood the power of food to spark memories and make you feel at home. I saw how the cuisine carries the culture. Never again would I question why my mother went to such lengths to replicate Hanoian recipes abroad. Through her cooking she rooted us in family tradition.

That afternoon, my mother went to the hairdresser and got her hair done in the exact same style she wore in those old black and white photos of her hanging on the wall at home. Suddenly she seemed as youthful as me, in her twenties with everything ahead of her. The sweetness of that day still lingers.

Everyday Cooking
(An Com)

The Vietnamese don't eat their meals in the sequential order of starter, main course, and dessert. At mealtimes the dishes are laid out together and everyone is called to the table. However simple the meal, the trinity of a protein main course, a vegetable side, and a soup is honored. The nurturer of the family, whether it be the mother or the eldest son, is given the important task of serving everyone rice, and typically two bowls are mandatory. Fruits and tea are served afterward. This traditional Vietnamese format is designed for communal dining. But you can pick out any dish you fancy from the following recipes and enjoy it alone. Or pick any selection to enjoy together with friends and family.

■ ■ ■ ■

Shrimp and Vegetable Marrow Squash Soup

SERVES 2

For the shrimp:

1 teaspoon freshly ground black
   pepper

1 tablespoon fish sauce

½ teaspoon chopped garlic

7 ounces/200 g fresh peeled
   shrimp, coarsely chopped

For the soup:

1 (7-ounce/200-g) chunk of
   vegetable marrow squash
   (zucchini also works well)

1 tablespoon vegetable oil

½ teaspoon crushed garlic

3 cups/750 ml hot water

1 teaspoon gia vi (or a mix
   of 2 parts sugar, 1 part sea salt,
   1 part ground black pepper,
   1 part garlic powder)

2 tablespoons fish sauce

1 spring onion, finely sliced,
   for serving

Soup forms an indispensable part of the Vietnamese meal. It's served together with the main course, usually poured over rice. We make easy, everyday soups from the simplest of ingredients: we boil a vegetable from the fridge, add a pinch of sea salt, muddle in a tomato or a few slices of ginger, and voila. The natural sweetness of many vegetables makes them the mainstay of a comforting soup. Vegetable marrow, a light green summer squash, is one of our favorite squashes, and one of the most dependable vegetables. We use it a chunk at a time, like a good piece of farmhouse Cheddar, and the squash lasts us a whole week. In this recipe, you can substitute zucchini just as well.

To prepare the shrimp: Combine the black pepper, fish sauce, and garlic in a medium bowl and toss with the shrimp. Cover and leave to marinate for a couple of minutes while you prepare the soup.

To prepare the soup: Peel the squash, cut it in half lengthways, and remove any seeds. Then use a vegetable peeler to slice the squash into paper-thin slices.

In a heavy-bottomed pan, heat the oil over medium-high heat, then stir in the garlic until the oil is fragrant. Pour in the marinated shrimp and stir quickly until they turn pink.

Pour in the hot water and bring to a boil, skimming off any foam that builds up. Season with the gia vi and the fish sauce, and add the squash slices. Cook for about 5 minutes, or until the squash is soft.

Take the pot off the heat and sprinkle with the chopped spring onion before serving.

Note: If you want the broth to be extra-sweet, then buy unpeeled shrimp to peel yourself. Cook the shells separately in the hot water for 5 to 10 minutes. Strain out the shells before adding the water to the sautéed shrimp.

Asparagus and Crabmeat Soup

SERVES 4

6⅓ cups/1.5 L chicken broth
   (see page 211, or use store-bought)
1 tablespoon vegetable oil
1 tablespoon chopped shallot
3½ ounces/100 g fresh white
   crabmeat
1 teaspoon fish sauce
2 tablespoons corn flour
4 tablespoons cold water
1 bunch asparagus
1¾ ounces/50 g fresh
   shiitake mushrooms
   (or ¾ ounce/20 g dried)
Freshly ground black pepper, to taste
2 tablespoons chopped fresh
   cilantro, for garnish

We are big fans of asparagus. In late spring, when asparagus is plentiful at the market, we pick up a couple of bunches every week. It is so versatile: we boil it with a dash of ginger, make a stir-fry (page 178), or pan-fry it lightly with a smidgen of butter, a dash of lemon juice, and a sprinkling of sesame. Asparagus and crabmeat scream luxurious cooking, but the truth is that you need only use a modest amount of each to create a big splash.

In a large pan, bring the chicken broth to a boil.

Meanwhile, prepare the components of the soup: In a separate, heavy-bottomed pan, heat the oil over medium-high heat, then stir in the chopped shallot, stirring quickly until the oil is fragrant, 1 to 2 minutes. Add the crabmeat and flash-fry for a couple of minutes, before seasoning with the fish sauce; stir to incorporate. Remove the pan from the heat.

In a small bowl, dissolve the corn flour in the cold water.

Chop the asparagus into ½-inch/1-cm rounds. Slice the shiitake mushrooms thinly. (If using dried shiitake, soak them in hot water for about 15 minutes, drain, and then pat them dry with a paper towel before slicing.)

Once the chicken broth is boiling, add the seasoned crabmeat, along with the asparagus and shiitake mushrooms. Return the broth to a boil and stir in the corn flour mixture. Stir for a couple of minutes until the soup thickens, and then take the pot off the heat.

Grind some fresh pepper over the soup and sprinkle the chopped cilantro over top before serving.

Grind some more pepper over the individual servings before eating.

Artichoke and Pork Ribs Soup

SERVES 2

10 ounces/300 g small pork loin ribs, cut into smallish pieces (see note)

6 whole fresh artichoke hearts

1 teaspoon gia vi (or a mix of 2 parts sugar, 1 part sea salt, 1 part ground black pepper, 1 part garlic powder)

2 teaspoons fish sauce

1 teaspoon chopped spring onion, for serving

1 teaspoon chopped fresh cilantro, for serving

When a vegetable as aristocratic as the artichoke is combined with something as common as pork ribs, the resulting sweetness is wonderfully ethereal.

Bring a large pan of water to a boil and add the pork ribs. Boil for a couple of minutes only, then drain and discard the liquid. (This is to cleanse the ribs, so don't cook for too long as they will lose their sweetness.)

Put the ribs back into the pan. Add enough water to come about 2 inches/5 cm above the ribs and bring to a boil again. Reduce the heat to medium-low and cook for 25 to 30 minutes, or until the ribs are tender.

Add the artichokes and cook until soft, 10 to 15 minutes. Stir in the gia vi along with the fish sauce.

Sprinkle with the chopped spring onion and cilantro and serve hot

Note: Ask the butcher to chop the ribs into small chunks for easier eating.

Chicken, Cauliflower, and Spring Onion Soup

SERVES 4

6⅓ cups/1.5 L chicken broth
  (see page 211 or use store-bought)
½ head cauliflower
1 teaspoon gia vi (or a mix
  of 2 parts sugar, 1 part sea salt,
  1 part ground black pepper,
  1 part garlic powder)
2 teaspoons fish sauce
1 tablespoon chopped spring onion
1 teaspoon chopped fresh
  cilantro

Often when we have a good chicken broth on hand we like to make a pho noodle soup (see page 46). On grey autumn evenings, however, we go for a really plain, clear soup. It is both simple and soothing.

In a large pan, bring the chicken broth to the boil. Cut the cauliflower into florets, add them to the broth, and cook until they are soft. Season to taste with the gia vi and fish sauce.

Sprinkle the chopped spring onion and cilantro over the broth and serve hot.

Pumpkin Braised with Coconut

SERVES 2

1 9-ounce/250-g pumpkin or
    other winter squash, peeled and
    deseeded
1 tablespoon vegetable oil
½ tablespoon chopped shallot
2 tablespoons soy sauce
6 tablespoons/100 ml
    coconut milk
1 tablespoon chopped
    spring onion
1 tablespoon chopped fresh cilantro,
    for serving

Throughout winter we always have pumpkins and winter squash in our vegetable box in the kitchen. We often slice them thinly and then stir-fry with lots of crushed garlic. But after they've been sitting in the vegetable box for some time their flesh begins to dry out, so we discovered that you could remedy that by cutting them into thick chunks and cooking them like a curry with coconut milk. Coconut milk injects the pumpkin with moisture and brings the flavors back to life.

Cut the pumpkin into bite-size chunks.

In a heavy-bottomed pan, heat the oil over medium-high heat and toss in the shallot. Cook for about 1 minute, until it starts to brown. Stir in the pumpkin and season with the soy sauce, then add just enough water to cover the pumpkin. Simmer over medium heat until the pumpkin is soft, which should take about 15 minutes. Pour in the coconut milk and simmer for another 15 minutes, to meld all the flavors.

Sprinkle the spring onion and cilantro on top before serving.

Egg-glazed Eggplant Fritters

SERVES 2

1 medium-size eggplant
1 egg
1 teaspoon fish sauce
1 tablespoon vegetable oil

On Saturday nights, after spending the whole day selling street food on Broadway Market, we are usually so tired and half-full from grazing on food we've swapped with the other traders, that all we want to cook is something simple like these eggplant fritters. We first thought of using tempura batter, which works for any vegetable, from cauliflower to zucchini slices, but then we made our batter even more simple by literally just cracking an egg, whisking with a fork, and dipping the thinly sliced eggplant into it. We munch on them as they come out of the pan, savoring the rich sweetness of the egg and the softness of the eggplant.

Cut the eggplant in half lengthwise and then cut each half into very thin (¼-inch-/2- or 3-mm-thick) slices.

In a small bowl, whisk the egg and season it with the fish sauce.

Heat the oil in a frying pan over medium-high heat.

Dip the eggplant slices in the egg, one at a time, and then immediately add the coated slices to the pan; fry until golden on both sides. Carefully remove the fried eggplant pieces to a plate lined with paper towels to drain. Serve warm.

Caramelized Braised Pork Belly

SERVES 4

2 thick slices peeled fresh ginger
10½ ounces/300 g pork belly

For the marinade:
1 tablespoon gia vi (or a mix
   of 2 parts sugar, 1 part sea salt,
   1 part ground black pepper,
   1 part garlic powder)
2 tablespoons fish sauce
1 teaspoon chopped shallot

For the caramel sauce:
4 teaspoons granulated sugar
1 scant cup/200 ml hot water
1 scant cup/200 ml canned
   coconut milk

My father was born in the countryside and although he's now a scientist with two doctorates, he has retained a penchant for simple, country comfort food. He loves leftover rice fried with greens, or sticky rice with caramelized pork. As my father completed his studies in Germany, I didn't meet him until I was three, but I inherited from him a love of caramelized pork. It's a staple dish at our kitchen table, especially in the winter months. In this recipe, the slow simmering of the pork makes it deliciously sweet and tender.

Bring a large pot of water to a boil over high heat and throw in the ginger. Add the pork (don't cut it into chunks at this stage or it will cook too quickly and lose its sweetness) and cook for about 3 to 4 minutes over a high heat to blanch the meat. Remove the pork belly from the pot and set it aside on a cutting board. Drain and discard the water and ginger.

For the marinade, mix together the gia vi, fish sauce, and shallot in a medium bowl. Slice the pork belly into bite-size chunks, add them to the marinade, and toss to coat. Cover the bowl and let it sit at room temperature for at least 15 minutes.

To make the caramel sauce, pour the sugar into a heavy-bottomed braising pan or cast-iron casserole. Place the pan over medium heat for 2 to 3 minutes without stirring, and then reduce the heat and stir constantly until the sugar is completely melted and begins to turn golden in color. This should take about 2 to 3 minutes. Pay attention to the color of the caramel underneath the bubbles: don't allow it to get too dark. Add the hot water and cook until it boils, and then immediately reduce the heat to medium and add the pork belly to the pan. Don't worry if the sugar hardens upon contact with the water; it will re-melt as it cooks, forming a sauce.

Stir the pork belly into the caramel sauce until it is well coated. Pour in the coconut milk, stir until it is incorporated, and cook the mixture for another minute to let the flavors meld. Taste and add more fish sauce or sugar if necessary, depending on whether it's a little too sweet or too salty.

Reduce the heat to low, cover, and leave the meat to simmer for about 30 minutes, until the braising liquid has reduced and thickened. Add a bit of water if the sauce reduces too much.

This is best served with white rice and a sour salad like the Red Cabbage and Bean Sprout Salad on page 92, which cuts through its sweetness.

Beef au Vin
(Bo Sot Vang)

SERVES 4

For the marinade:

6½ tablespoons/100 ml red wine
1 tablespoon gia vi (or a mix
 of 2 parts sugar, 1 part sea salt,
 1 part ground black pepper,
 1 part garlic powder)
2 tablespoons fish sauce
½ teaspoon ground cinnamon
2 tablespoons granulated sugar
1 tablespoon grated fresh ginger
1 teaspoon crushed garlic

For the stew:

2¼ pounds/1 kg diced stewing beef
3 medium-size tomatoes
1 generous quart/1 L boiling water
1 cinnamon stick
1 star anise
7 ounces/200 g carrots,
 peeled and trimmed

Beef was not part of the Vietnamese diet until the French arrived in the late nineteenth century and started to import it. Although there were buffalos in Vietnam, they were work animals only and designated as holy.

Like most French dishes that came to Vietnam, this recipe changed en route, and the beef stew is now spiced with strong flavors like cinnamon and star anise. We love this recipe, which we got from friends in New York, because it feels sumptuous yet comforting. When we're feeling weary all we need is to be fed a bowl of warm, sweet, and perfectly spiced stew.

Place the marinade ingredients in a large bowl and mix well. Add the diced beef to the bowl and rub it in the marinade with your hands. Cover and leave the bowl in the fridge for at least 30 minutes.

Cut each tomato in half and then slice each half into thirds.

Put a heavy-bottomed pan over medium-high heat. Once it's hot, add the beef and its marinade and cook, stirring constantly, so the beef does not burn. After 5 to 10 minutes, reduce the heat to medium-low, add the tomatoes, and simmer for another 10 minutes until they are soft.

Add up to 1 generous quart/1 L boiling water to the pan (enough to just cover the meat), along with the cinnamon stick and star anise. Bring to a boil, then reduce the heat to low. Simmer for at least 45 minutes or until the beef is fully cooked. Check on the beef every now and then and add more water if it has reduced too much.

Cut the carrots into pieces about ½ inch/1 cm thick. Add the carrot pieces to the pan and simmer until they are soft and ready to eat, about 15 minutes. Fish out the cinnamon stick and star anise before serving.

Note: We tend to eat this stew very simply with a fresh baguette. It is also great with rice or potatoes. You can make this recipe with oxtail, too—just double the stewing time.

Festive Cooking
(An Qua)

Festive cooking in Vietnam falls into two categories. The first is the multi-course banquet served at public occasions like weddings, wakes, anniversaries, birthdays, and events to honor elders or even ancestors. Traditional dishes like spring rolls are beautifully arranged on platters, and the extended family and neighbors (which in the country means the whole village) are wined and dined. The second type of festive cooking is at more intimate family celebrations like Sundays at the grandparents' and weekend family dinners.

It's the occasion to make a large pot of wonderful and complexly seasoned broth that will serve many bowls of noodle soups, allowing the host to pour the bubbling broths over prepared bowls as friends and relatives arrive in groups. Watching adults and children alike sit down to slurp the sweetness of the noodle soup is probably the most loving act of communal dining.

■ ■ ■ ■

Imperial BBQ Pork

SERVES 4

2¼ pounds/1 kg boneless
   pork shoulder

For the marinade:
1 tablespoon finely chopped shallot
1 tablespoon finely chopped
   spring onion
1 teaspoon crushed garlic
4 tablespoons fish sauce
½ tablespoon salt
½ tablespoon freshly ground
   black pepper
1 tablespoon finely chopped
   lemongrass
4 tablespoons granulated sugar
¼ tablespoon ground chile powder
1 cup/240 ml caramel water
   (see page 212)

Here we have adapted a traditional Hanoian marinade by adding lemongrass and chile, the signature spices of the imperial city, Hue. This pork is perfect served with vermicelli noodles and an herb salad (page 42). We also use it in our banh mi baguettes (page 40), and it is the most popular filling at our stall. You can also serve it in a summer roll (page 185).

Slice the pork shoulder thinly into about ⅛-inch/2-mm slices. The thinner you slice the meat, the better it will absorb the flavors in this recipe.

For the marinade, in a large bowl combine the shallot, spring onion, garlic, fish sauce, salt, pepper, lemongrass, sugar, chile powder, and caramel water. Add the pork and mix well, rubbing the marinade in vigorously with your hands. Cover the bowl and leave it in the fridge for at least an hour before cooking, or ideally, overnight.

Preheat a grill on high heat. Thread the pork onto skewers and grill for 10 to 15 minutes, turning frequently.

Note: You can cook this on a barbecue grill or in the oven. For the latter, put the skewers on a rack over a foil-lined baking tray so the oil can drip through, then cook in a 350°F/180°C/gas 4 oven for about 25 to 30 minutes, until browned. The traditional Vietnamese way of cooking the pork is on a metal grill "net" (see photo opposite). You can buy nets in Asian supermarkets. Spread the pork in a layer over the net and put the net on the grill or in a very hot oven. Because the pork is in a single layer it chars on the outside without drying out in the middle.

To slice the meat thinly; you can part-freeze it first (see page 231).

Basic Vietnamese Baguette
(Banh Mi)

MAKES 1

1 tablespoon country pâté
1 teaspoon unsalted butter
1 demi-baguette
1 teaspoon mayonnaise
1 squirt chili sauce
1 fresh chile, chopped
   (like Thai or another fruity chile)
3 to 4 slices cucumber
2 to 3 sprigs cilantro

A banh mi combines a variety of individual ingredients in a baguette. The filling could include anything from barbecued pork to grilled fish, topped with pickles and fresh herbs to create a culinary delight. Here we give you the "essential" banh mi, pared down to the key ingredients you won't want to do without.

Preheat the oven to 350°F/180°C/gas 4.

In a small pan, melt the pâté with the unsalted butter, or put the pâté and butter in a small microwave-safe bowl and microwave the mixture for about 1 minute so it is warm and spreadable.

Split the baguette lengthways—you might need to remove some of the doughy filling inside.

Smear a layer of mayo on the top half of the baguette—just enough to moisten the bread without drenching it—and spread the melted pâté on the bottom half.

Close the baguette and toast it in the oven for 3 to 5 minutes, so the inside is warm and the outside is crispy. Take care not to burn it.

Remove the baguette from the oven, using tongs or chopsticks, and flip it open. Spread a little chili sauce on the pâté and scatter some chopped chile on top. Arrange slices of cucumber and sprigs of cilantro neatly along the baguette. Close the baguette and use a small knife to push all the ingredients inside. Serve right away.

Imperial BBQ Pork Vietnamese Baguette (*Banh Mi*)

MAKES 1

1 teaspoon country pâté
½ teaspoon unsalted butter
1 demi-baguette
1 teaspoon mayonnaise
Carrot and Daikon Pickles,
   as desired (see page 215)
3 to 3½ ounces/80 to 100 g
   Imperial BBQ Pork (see page 36)
1 squirt chili sauce, or to taste
1 fresh chile, chopped
   (like Thai or another fruity chile)
3 to 4 slices cucumber
2 to 3 sprigs cilantro

Each of the ingredients in a banh mi is potentially a recipe in itself, and at Banhmi11 we make everything from scratch. Luckily, these days you can buy nearly all the ingredients ready to go. If you have a good farmers' market near you, get hold of some proper butter, pâté de campagne, and of course a crisp baguette. It's also worth hunting down authentic chili sauce from an Asian grocer. Perhaps the only thing we would encourage you to spend extra time on is home-made pickles, which add a mouthwatering sourness and crunch to your banh mi.

Preheat the oven to 350°F/180°C/gas 4.

In a small pan, melt the pâté with the butter, or put the pate and butter in a small microwave-safe bowl and microwave the mixture for about 1 minute so it is warm and spreadable.

Split the baguette lengthways—you might need to remove some of the doughy filling inside.

Smear a layer of mayo on the top half of the baguette—just enough to moisten the bread without drenching it—and spread the melted pâté on the bottom half.

Close the baguette and toast it in the oven for 3 to 5 minutes so the inside is warm and the outside is crispy. Take care not to burn the bread.

Remove the baguette from the oven, using tongs or chopsticks, and flip it open. Add a thin layer of Carrot and Daikon Pickles on the pâté—squeezing out any pickle brine first so the bread stays dry and crisp—then top with the grilled pork. Spread a little chili sauce on the meat and scatter some chopped chile on top. Arrange slices of cucumber and sprigs of cilantro neatly along the baguette. Close the baguette and use a small knife to push all the ingredients inside. Serve right away.

Imperial BBQ Pork Noodle Salad
(*Bun Cha*)

SERVES 4

1 (14-ounce/400-g) pack dried
   rice vermicelli noodles
7 ounces/200 g Imperial BBQ
   Pork (see page 36)
2 cups/100 g bean sprouts
4 tablespoons Carrot and Daikon
   Pickles (see page 215),
   or to taste
Small bunch of mint, chopped
Garlic, Lime and Chile Dipping
   Sauce (see page 218)
Freshly ground black pepper

Anh's mother is a woman of many talents. Now well into her seventies, she still rides her faithful old '82 Honda scooter fearlessly round Hanoi's rush hour, carrying Anh on the back through snaking queues of traffic. She has done a lot of things in her life, and most of them had something to do with food. Anh's first memory is of helping her mum seal bags of roast peanuts to sell. When Anh was very little, her mother retired from teaching and set up a noodle salad or *bun cha* stall, which was the first in a string of stalls. She rented a small space on the pavement near Anh's nursery school—a treat for people travelling on the main road out from Hanoi.

Cook the noodles according to the packet instructions and drain thoroughly. Then tip the noodles into each of four bowls: they should fill a quarter or a third of each bowl, depending on how hungry you are.

Arrange the meat on top of the noodles. Garnish with the bean sprouts, pickles, and mint.

To serve, whisk together the Garlic, Lime and Chile Dipping Sauce and drizzle over each bowl to taste. Finish with some black pepper.

Classic Beef Noodle Soup
(Pho Bo)

SERVES 4

For the steak:

14 ounces/400 g sirloin steak

1 tablespoon grated fresh ginger

1 tablespoon fish sauce

1 teaspoon gia vi (or a mix
  of 2 parts sugar, 1 part sea salt,
  1 part ground black pepper,
  1 part garlic powder)

For the broth:

8½ cups/2 L beef broth (see page
  210, or use store-bought)

2 garlic cloves

2 star anise

2 cardamom pods

1 cinnamon stick

1 large red onion, unpeeled

110-ounce/300-g piece fresh
  ginger, unpeeled

2 tablespoons gia vi (or a mix
  of 2 parts sugar, 1 part sea salt,
  1 part ground black pepper,
  1 part garlic powder)

2 tablespoons fish sauce

1 tablespoon packed
  brown sugar

A truly authentic beef pho takes time to make. We cook ours for more than 72 hours! But if you're cooking for the family, you can do everything in a day and you will have amazing pho for dinner. The broth, with the added spices, can be prepared in advance; it will keep in the fridge for a couple of days, or it can be frozen and kept for a couple of weeks in the freezer. Apart from the meat preparation, pho pretty much cooks itself, which is why it's perfect for big festive gatherings.

To prepare the steak: Slice the sirloin steak very thinly. Combine the grated ginger, fish sauce, and gia vi in a large bowl and add the steak slices, turning to coat them in the marinade. Cover the bowl and leave it on the counter to marinate while you prepare the rest of the ingredients.

To make the broth: In a large pan or stockpot, bring the beef broth to a boil and add the garlic cloves, star anise, cardamom pods, and cinnamon. Simmer over low heat while you prepare the onion and ginger.

If you have a gas stove, turn one of your burners to high flame. If you have an electric stove, preheat the broiler to high. Char the onion and ginger over the open flame or under the broiler for about 15 minutes, using tongs to rotate them occasionally, until their skins burn and they become soft and fragrant. Alternatively, you can grill them for 15 minutes, turning them halfway through. Remove the charred skins, wash the onion and ginger, and add them whole to the broth.

Simmer the broth for 30 minutes longer, and then pick out and discard the onion, ginger and whole spices.

Add the gia vi, fish sauce, and brown sugar; taste and add salt or sugar as necessary.

For the pho bowls:
1 to 2 (14-ounce/400-g) packs
   dried pho noodles
4 tablespoons finely chopped
   spring onions
1 bunch cilantro, finely chopped
2 teaspoons fish sauce
Freshly ground black pepper

To serve:
4 lime wedges
1 to 2 fresh chiles, or to taste,
   chopped

To assemble the pho bowls: Cook the rice noodles according to the packet instructions, then drain and tip the noodles into your bowls. They should fill a quarter or a third of each bowl, depending on your preference.

Drain the meat and discard the marinade. Arrange the meat on the noodles. Garnish with the spring onion and cilantro. Add ½ teaspoon of fish sauce to each bowl and finish with black pepper to taste.

Bring the broth to a bubbling boil. Plunge the ladle deeply to the bottom of the pot, where the broth is hottest, and ladle into each bowl, distributing it evenly so it cooks the raw meat and warms the other ingredients.

The meat will be cooked but rare, so if you prefer your meat more well done, flash-fry the meat before adding it to your bowls. To flash-fry the meat, heat 1 tablespoon of oil in a medium skillet over medium-high heat. Add 1 teaspoon of minced garlic to the skillet, cook for a minute or two until fragrant, then add the meat strips, fry them for a few seconds, and immediately remove them from the pan to the bowls.

Serve the pho with wedges of lime and fresh chile to taste.

Note: When you add the fish sauce to the pho broth, pour a small quantity into a ladle and slowly dip the ladle in the broth in a circular motion until the ladle is fully submerged. This ensures that the pungent fish sauce smell disperses so it doesn't overwhelm the dish.

Classic Chicken Noodle Soup
(Pho Ga)

SERVES 4

For the broth:
8½ cups/2 L chicken broth
   (see page 211, or use store-bought)
2 garlic cloves
2 star anise
2 cardamom pods
1 cinnamon stick
1 large red onion, unpeeled
10 ounces/300 g piece fresh ginger,
   unpeeled
2 tablespoons gia vi (or a mix
   of 2 parts sugar, 1 part sea salt,
   1 part ground black pepper,
   1 part garlic powder)
2 tablespoons fish sauce
1 tablespoon brown sugar

My mother told me that in the fifties there was no beef on Mondays and Fridays, and this is why chicken pho was invented. Some pho fanatics considered it sacrilege while others warmed to the lighter sweetness of chicken pho broth. The debate between followers of beef and chicken pho still rages. The chicken pho camp consider it more sophisticated, with its clear broth, thinly shredded white meat, and long strips of spring onion. For the best flavor, use a boiler chicken, which you can often find at halal butchers. Otherwise, buy free-range chickens from the farmers' market. Or do as we do and just buy a chicken carcass (we buy ours from Matthew at Broadway Market): nobody wants them and they make terrific stocks.

To make the broth: In a large pan or stockpot over medium-high heat, bring the chicken broth to a boil and add the garlic cloves, star anise, cardamom pods, and cinnamon. Reduce the heat to low and let the broth simmer while you prepare the onion and ginger.

If you have a gas stove, turn one of your burners to high flame. If you have an electric stove, preheat the broiler to high. Char the onion and ginger over the open flame or under the broiler for about 15 minutes, using tongs to rotate them occasionally, until their skins burn and they become soft and fragrant. Alternatively, you can grill them for 15 minutes, turning them halfway through. Remove the charred skin, wash the onion and ginger, and add them whole to the broth.

Simmer the broth for 30 minutes longer, then pick out and discard the onion, ginger, and whole spices. Add the gia vi, fish sauce, and brown sugar; taste and adjust with more salt or sugar as necessary.

For the pho bowls:

1 to 2 (14-ounce/400-g) packs
   dried pho noodles

14 ounces/400 g shredded
   cooked chicken

2 large bunches spring onions,
   finely chopped

1 bunch cilantro, finely chopped

2 teaspoons fish sauce

Freshly ground black pepper

To serve:

4 lime wedges

1 to 2 fresh chiles, or to taste,
   chopped

To assemble the pho bowls: Cook the noodles according to the packet instructions, then drain and tip the noodles into your bowls. They should fill a quarter or a third of each bowl, depending on your preference.

Arrange the shredded chicken on top of the noodles. Garnish with the spring onions and cilantro, add ½ teaspoon fish sauce to each bowl, and finish with some black pepper to taste.

Bring the broth to a bubbling boil. Check the seasoning one last time, adjusting if needed, then ladle the broth into each bowl, distributing it evenly. Serve with wedges of lime and fresh chile to taste.

Note: When you add the fish sauce to the broth, pour a small quantity into a ladle and slowly dip the ladle in the broth in a circular motion until the ladle is fully submerged. This ensures that the pungent fish sauce smell disperses so it doesn't overwhelm the dish.

Classic Chicken Noodle Soup
(Pho Ga), page 46

Classic Beef Noodle Soup
(Pho Bo), page 44

Stairway to Heaven Noodle Soup
(Bun Thang), page 50

Stairway to Heaven Noodle Soup
(Bun Thang)

SERVES 4

2 ounces/50 g dried shiitake
    mushrooms
2 tablespoons vegetable oil
1 large egg, beaten
3½ ounces/100 g Vietnamese pork
    ham (optional)

For the broth:
8½ cups/2 L chicken broth
    (see page 211, or use store-bought)
2 tablespoons gia vi (or a mix
    of 2 parts sugar, 1 part sea salt,
    1 part ground black pepper,
    1 part garlic powder)
2 tablespoons fish sauce
1 tablespoon packed brown sugar
1 tablespoon diluted shrimp paste
    (page 231)

I had my first bowl of bun thang in third grade. Our teacher ran a half-day boarding scheme at her house, where we would receive extra teaching in the morning, eat lunch made by her mother, and then be transported to our formal afternoon classes on cyclos. I remember thinking: I don't want to move on to the next grade.

Bun is a noodle made from rice. *Thang* is understood to come from the word "tang," meaning "soup" in Chinese. In Vietnamese, *thang* means "stairs," so it reminds us of the many steps required to construct this noodle soup. At Banhmi11, we call this the "stairway to heaven soup." Bun thang is typical of Hanoi cuisine: it uses no spicy flavors like lemongrass or chile, but still achieves a fantastically complex taste.

Soak the dried shiitakes in warm water until soft, at least 10 minutes, depending on how dry the mushrooms are. Drain and discard the water, and let them dry for a few minutes before slicing them into small thin strips.

Heat the oil in a wok or frying pan over medium heat and pour in the beaten egg. Fry the egg in a thin layer, without stirring, until it is cooked through, 1 to 3 minutes. Remove the cooked egg from the pan and place it on a cutting board. Let the egg cool for a few minutes, then slice it into long thin strips.

Prepare the pork ham by slicing it into long thin strips.

To make the broth: Bring the chicken broth to a boil in a large pot. Turn the heat down to low and add the gia vi, fish sauce, and brown sugar. Stir in the diluted shrimp paste (prepared as on page 231).

Taste the broth and adjust with more salt or sugar as necessary.

For the bun thang bowls:

1 to 2 (14-ounce/400-g) packs
   dried rice vermicelli noodles

14 ounces/400 g shredded
   cooked chicken

7 ounces/200 g cooked king shrimp

4 tablespoons finely chopped
   spring onions

1 small bunch rau ram or cilantro,
   finely chopped

2 teaspoons fish sauce

Freshly ground black pepper

To assemble the bun thang bowls: Cook the noodles according to the packet instructions and divide among your bowls. Each bowl will be filled by a quarter or a third, depending on your preference. Arrange the shredded chicken and shrimp (and the slices of Vietnamese pork ham, if using) on top of the noodles.

Divide the shiitake mushrooms and fried egg strips between the bowls.

Sprinkle the spring onions and chopped herbs over the meat. Add ½ teaspoon of fish sauce to each bowl and finish with black pepper to taste.

Bring the broth to a bubbling boil and ladle it into each bowl, distributing it evenly.

Note: Another authentic ingredient you can include in this dish is shrimp floss. Take 2 ounces/50 g dried shrimp and soak them in hot water for 20 minutes. Then mince the shrimp in a blender or food processor until very flaky. Put a wok over medium heat and add the minced shrimp. Stir continuously with a wooden spoon for 5 to 10 minutes until the shrimp is dry. Transfer the shrimp to a plate and let it cool before adding to the bowls along with the meat.

Social Cooking

(An Choi)

Eating in Vietnam is almost always a social event. Sometimes it feels as if all social activities there are centered around food! There is shopping at the market; whizzing on scooters to catch the street-food vendors who pitch up for an hour a day with just one type of dish; and sitting in cafés, sipping cups of Vietnamese coffee.

Social food tends to be in smaller and lighter portions, but it usually packs a flavorful punch. There's scope for imagination when it comes to shared plates, snacks, and sweets. Nature plays its part here, not only in the scent and color of ingredients, but also in their presentation. In Vietnam sticky rice is wrapped in earthy lotus leaves, beef is grilled on lemongrass skewers, and fish is folded in fragrant banana leaves. Sticks of sugar cane make delicious substitutes for metal skewers, lending sweetness to recipes like barbecued shrimps. For dessert or a teatime snack we usually have fresh fruit, or sometimes a pudding like crème caramel.

■ ■ ■ ■

Shrimp Lollipops

SERVES 4

18 ounces/500 g tiger shrimp,
  fresh or frozen, peeled
  and deveined

3 teaspoons fish sauce,
  plus 1 teaspoon for serving

1 teaspoon freshly ground black
  pepper, plus a pinch for serving

1 teaspoon granulated sugar

1 teaspoon crushed garlic

3 tablespoons/50 ml annatto seed
  oil (see page 209) or vegetable
  oil, divided

Vegetable oil for frying

1 spring onion

15 to 20 sugar cane sticks
  for assembling pops (optional)

We cooked these shrimp pops at our first-ever supper club. We held our pop-up at F. Cooke, the eel and mash shop on Broadway Market, and the electricity went on the blink every five minutes! For an authentic Vietnamese presentation, mold the pops onto sticks of sugar cane or lemongrass rather than metal skewers.

You can prepare the pops a day in advance and keep them in the fridge, then quickly fry them before your guests arrive. They can be served as an appetizer or party finger food, or as a main course with vermicelli noodles and a dipping sauce.

Grind the shrimp into a paste in a food processor with 3 teaspoons of fish sauce, 1 teaspoon of pepper, and the sugar and garlic.

Mix 2 teaspoons of the annatto seed oil into the paste.

Tip the paste into a bowl. Using a firm hand, stir the paste with a silicone spatula for a couple of minutes, pressing it against the sides until it is dough-like with a spongy consistency.

Scoop out a spoonful of paste at a time, and flatten it out in the palm of your hand. Then put a sugar cane stick in the middle, and by clenching your hand, wrap the paste around the stick until it looks like a popsicle. Be careful not to make it too big so that the paste can cook easily.

Use the same process with more sticks until you have used up all the paste.

Use a pastry brush to brush a small amount of annatto seed oil on the outside of each pop.

Add about 1 scant inch/2 cm of vegetable oil to a frying pan—just enough to cover and shallow-fry the pops. Put the pan over medium-low heat and, when the oil is hot, gently fry the shrimp pops, a few at a time, for a couple of minutes until the outside is a nice golden color.

Finely chop the spring onion and place it in a small bowl. In a small frying pan over medium-high heat, warm the remaining 2 tablespoons of annatto seed oil and pour it over the spring onion. Add the remaining teaspoon of fish sauce and a pinch of freshly ground black pepper to the bowl and toss to combine. Arrange the shrimp pops on a plate and drizzle the spring onion oil over them to serve.

Note: Frozen, ready-cut sugar cane sticks are available in the large Vietnamese or Asian supermarkets. If you can't find them, use metal skewers or fresh lemongrass sticks.

Crab Cakes

SERVES 4
AS A STARTER

11 ounces/300 g ground pork

18 ounces/50 g fresh white
  crabmeat

1 tablespoon chopped shallots

2 teaspoons crushed garlic

2 teaspoons gia vi (or a mix
  of 2 parts granulated sugar,
  1 part sea salt, 1 part ground black
  pepper, 1 part garlic powder)

1 tablespoon fish sauce

1 teaspoon granulated sugar

1 teaspoon freshly ground
  black pepper

2 tablespoons water

2 teaspoons vegetable oil,
  plus more as needed

1 egg

4 ounces/125 g com rice
  (optional: see note)

This basic crab cake recipe makes for an easy and tasty snack. But we can't resist experimenting, so in the note below we've explained how you can add an authentic textured crust. The secret ingredient is com, a specialty found only in Hanoi, only in September, and from one single village alone! Com is sweet, young, green rice, harvested early; it is soft, bouncy, and immensely fragrant. It is brought into the city by vagrant vendors carrying baskets across their shoulders or on their bicycles. If you want to try this version, you can find com in Asian supermarkets and online.

In a bowl, mix the ground pork and crabmeat with the shallots, garlic, gia vi, fish sauce, sugar, and pepper. Add the water and 2 teaspoons of oil to the paste and continue mixing. Crack the egg and add it to the bowl, mixing well.

Using your hands, form the mixture into roughly 10 little patties.

In a frying pan or wok, heat about 1 scant inch/2 cm of oil over medium-high heat. When the oil is hot, gently fry the crab cakes in batches until golden, 3 to 5 minutes per side.

Note: If you want to make this with the young green com rice, soak the com in just enough hot water to cover. After about 10 minutes the rice will be plump and should have soaked up most of the water. Drain the rice of any remaining water. Mix half of the rice into the meat mixture and spread the other half out on a flat surface to roll the patties in before frying them.

Chinese Leaf Pork Dumplings

Pork dumplings wrapped in cabbage leaves are one of my mother's oldest recipes. I ate this dish every winter as a child in Hanoi. Even when I moved abroad, my mother still made it every winter holiday when I flew home. Now when I miss my mother, I cook these dumplings.

In this recipe, we've used Chinese cabbage for its sweetness and softness, but savoy cabbage works just as well.

**SERVES 4
AS A STARTER**

1 Chinese cabbage (or substitute with Savoy cabbage)
3½ ounces/100 g chestnut mushrooms
7 ounces/200 g ground pork
1 teaspoon chopped garlic
1 teaspoon chopped shallot
1 teaspoon freshly ground black pepper
1 tablespoon fish sauce
Chili sauce, to serve

Separate the whole leaves from the cabbage.

In a steamer (or a metal colander or steamer basket set over a pan of simmering water), lightly steam the leaves so they are soft and foldable but not overcooked, 5 to 7 minutes.

Finely chop the chestnut mushrooms and place them in a medium bowl. Mix in the pork, garlic, shallot, pepper, and fish sauce.

On a chopping board or clean surface, lay out the steamed Chinese cabbage leaves and cut into 3 x 4-inch (7.5 x 10-cm) rectangles. Spoon a teaspoon of the pork and mushroom mix into the middle of a single leaf, fold in the short sides, then roll the rest of the leaf over.

Repeat until you have used all of the mixture. It should make roughly 10 dumplings.

Cook the dumplings in a steamer (or a metal colander or steamer basket set over a pan of simmering water) for 5 to 8 minutes, until cooked. Cut open a dumpling to be sure the pork is cooked all the way through.

Serve the dumplings warm or cold with some chili sauce drizzled on top.

Pomegranate and Pear Sweet Pudding

SERVES 4

3 tablespoons tapioca flour
17 ounces/500 ml water
8 ounces/250 ml coconut milk
¾ cup/115 g granulated sugar
1 pomegranate
1 pear
Ice cubes, to serve (optional)

Vietnamese food is almost always dairy-free, as we use soy milk or coconut milk instead of cow's milk. So our desserts are quite different from Western ones. We have one typical pudding that we call *che*, which is usually tapioca bubbles simmered for a long time with fruit. We have made our recipe quicker and fresher by using simple tapioca flour as well as fresh fruit that hasn't been stewed to death. You can use just about any fruit— apple, pear, or mango— to achieve a mild, fragrant sweetness.

In a saucepan over medium-high heat, dissolve the tapioca flour in the water, add the coconut milk, and bring the mixture to a boil. Reduce the heat to medium-low, and stir in the sugar. Stir occasionally while you prep the fruit: it should gradually thicken.

Cut the pomegranate in half and remove the seeds. Peel and core the pear, then chop it into tiny pieces of a similar size to the pomegranate seeds.

Stir the fruit pieces into the tapioca and coconut milk mixture. Continue to cook on low heat for another 7 to 9 minutes. The fruit will soak up the liquid, but it won't be too soft.

Serve warm in a bowl, or let the pudding cool and serve it cold over ice.

Kumquat Jasmine Iced Tea

SERVES 2

12 kumquats, plus more
  kumquat slices for garnish
  (substitute 2 clementines)
3 tablespoons granulated sugar
  or honey
4 cups strong jasmine tea
  (substitute black tea if you prefer)
Crushed ice, to serve
2 mint leaves, for garnish

On one of the nights visiting New Spitafields Market, we picked up a box of kumquat fruits. These golden, fragrant citrus fruits have an honorable place in Vietnamese homes, together with cherry blossom branches, to celebrate the New Year. We were so excited to see these fruits that reminded us of the time of year when food, family, and festivities culminate in the three days of Tet celebration. Kumquats are tangy, juicy, and fragrant, and, best of all, even the skin is edible. If you cannot find kumquats, clementines work perfectly well.

This is a classic iced tea recipe we used to make at Banhmill's café in Shoreditch.

Cut the kumquats in half and use a fine-mesh sieve or citrus juicer to crush and squeeze the juice out. We are after both the juice and the fragrant oil that comes out from the skin. Pour the juice into a jar, and add the sugar and brewed tea. Mix well.

Add crushed ice to the pitcher. Garnish with the kumquat slices and mint leaves before serving over more ice.

Notes: Instead of using fresh kumquat juice, you can also cook the kumquats into a syrup to keep in the pantry. Use 1 part kumquats to 1 part sugar, by weight. Cut the kumquats in half, place them in a saucepan over low heat, and stir in the sugar. Keep stirring over low heat until the sugar melts and the juice from the kumquats oozes out, making a syrup. Cook for 30 minutes over very low heat and keep stirring constantly until the kumquat fruits have dried out and the syrup is thick and golden.

Crème Caramel

SERVES 6

1 (14-ounce/397-g) can
  condensed milk

2 cans' worth hot water
  (28 ounces/794 g measured in
  condensed milk can)

4 egg yolks

3 tablespoons granulated sugar

¾ teaspoon vanilla extract

¼ teaspoon salt

⅔ cup/150 ml Caramel Water
  (see page 212)

"Banhmily" is what we call our staff at Banhmi11. We are a group of workaholics and dreamers, on a somewhat chaotic mission, but somehow we manage to hold everything together, bound by our shared love of food.

This crème caramel recipe came from a challenge we set when testing recipes for our dinner menu. Anh would test a different savory recipe every day, while Tu Anh, her junior namesake, would test a dessert.

The condensed milk really brings out the sweetness in this dish, although fresh milk or cream works equally as well (add additional sugar to taste, if needed).

Preheat the oven to 355°F/180°C/gas 4.

Empty the condensed milk into a large bowl. Use the can to measure out two times this amount of hot water, and add it to the bowl. Stir so the condensed milk is mixed into the hot water.

In a small bowl, whisk together the egg yolks and sugar and pour the mixture into the milk, along with the vanilla and salt. Mix well.

Strain the mixture through a coarse mesh strainer lined with cheesecloth to remove any lumps, so that the liquid has a smooth, silky texture.

Divide the caramel water among 6 ramekins. Gently pour the condensed milk mixture on top of the Caramel Water in each of the ramekins, dividing it evenly.

Place the ramekins in a water bath (or in a roasting tin with enough hot water to come two-thirds of the way up the ramekins). Bake in the oven for 25 minutes or until set.

Remove the pan from the oven and allow the crème caramels to cool completely in the pan, and then put them in the fridge for about 2 hours to set. Serve cold.

SOURNESS
&
CHANGE

Chapter 2

The idea of a sour flavor might well bring to mind grimaces and sharp acidity. This is a misconception. It might not have the instant gratification of sweetness, but sourness is, in our opinion, the most nuanced flavor. There is the delightful light sourness of a Cox's apple, the fragrant freshness of lime, and the sharp acidity of vinegar, to name but a few. Sourness tempered with sweetness is widely used in Vietnamese cooking—from classic sweet and sour soup to zingy salads.

When Anh came to England to study at age 16, and when I moved to Sweden with my family at age 12, we experienced entirely new sour flavors: piquant Bramley apple crumbles, deceptively sour fragrant quinces, balsamic vinegar's sweet acidity, piercingly tart Swedish gherkins. All of these new taste sensations coincided with the upheaval of moving to a new school and a new country.

For us, sourness is the flavor of change. Change brings renewal, and when balanced with familiarity—like the marriage of sour with sweet—good things tend to happen. A midwinter red cabbage salad sprinkled with hot mint defies winter's dullness with its color and flavor (see page 92).

During our first year away from Vietnam, Anh and I endured terrible school meals and, for the first time, we realized the need to cook if we were to control our enjoyment of food. Nothing we saw, smelled, or tasted at school really satisfied us, and this hunger made cooking an obsession. We took change into our own hands.

Everyday Cooking
(An Com)

When Banhmi11 stopped feeling like a hobby and began demanding our full-time attention, Anh quit her job. No fanfare, just a quiet acceptance that sometimes we choose our vocation and sometimes it chooses us. We recruited our first interns, who helped out with the admin, and a lot more besides—removing trash, testing menus, ferreting out ingredients, and endlessly peeling garlic and squeezing lemon juice.

Crammed together in our kitchen-cum-office, we made lunch together. This was a daily exercise in improvisation. We stir-fried beef, instead of grilling it as on our market stall menu, and ate it over vermicelli noodles. When we had ribs left over from pork belly, we made broth and threw in left-over pineapple and tomatoes for a sweet and sour soup.

Our kitchen had only the most rudimentary equipment, the centerpiece of which was a secondhand Blue Seal oven and six-burner hob we picked up from a Turkish catering shop. All six burners were occupied with cooking pho broth or making banh mi fillings, so we had to use the electric rice cooker in the corner of the office. This turned out to be a useful lesson in the value of simple, everyday cooking methods.

We didn't expect the interns to come every day, but they did. We didn't expect to eat together every day, but we did. Today, those first interns still work with us and are some of our most valued staff.

■ ■ ■ ■

Rhubarb and Okra Sweet and Sour Soup

SERVES 4

3 rhubarb stalks
4 medium-size tomatoes
½ pineapple, peeled and cored
2 ounces/50 g fresh okra
1 tablespoon vegetable oil
1 teaspoon crushed garlic
1 teaspoon gia vi (or a mix
    of 2 parts sugar, 1 part sea salt,
    1 part ground black pepper,
    1 part garlic powder), divided
6¼ cups/1.5 L water
2 tablespoons fish sauce
1 teaspoon granulated sugar
1 tablespoon chopped spring onion
1 tablespoon chopped fresh
    cilantro

Rhubarb has always fascinated us. When we see its crimson stalks at the farmers' market, it's as if it's asking to be picked up. We love our rhubarb crumble and tarts, but recently we also found a way of making rhubarb into a sweet and sour soup. Anh was rummaging in the fridge for ingredients we could salvage, and she came across a few rhubarb stalks. On a whim we cut the stalks into chunks and tossed them into a soup. The results were so beautiful that we cooked the same soup three days in a row.

Cut the rhubarb into bite-size chunks. Slice the tomatoes in half and cut each half lengthways into 3 or 4 slices. Cut the pineapple into small chunks. Slice the okra into small rounds.

In a heavy-bottomed pan over medium-high heat, heat the oil and stir in the garlic until the oil is fragrant, about 1 minute, taking care not to burn the garlic. Stir in the tomatoes and season with ½ teaspoon of the gia vi. Pour in just enough of the water to cover the tomatoes, and bring to a boil.

When the tomatoes are soft, add the remaining water and bring the mixture back to a boil. Add the rhubarb and cook until very soft, about 12 to 15 minutes. Stir in the fish sauce, sugar, remaining gia vi, okra, and pineapple, and cook for 15 minutes more. Sprinkle with the spring onion and cilantro, and serve right away.

Sweet and Sour Ribs with Pineapple Sauce

SERVES 4

For the pork ribs:

1 cup/250 ml water

1 teaspoon salt

1 (generous 1-inch/3-cm) piece
　fresh ginger, peeled and sliced

2 pounds/1 kg pork loin ribs

1 tablespoon gia vi (or a mix
　of 2 parts sugar, 1 part sea salt,
　1 part ground black pepper,
　1 part garlic powder)

2 tablespoons fish sauce

½ tablespoon fresh lemon juice

7 tablespoons/100 ml fresh
　apple juice

½ tablespoon freshly ground
　black pepper

2½ tablespoons finely
　chopped garlic, divided

1 tablespoon plus 2 teaspoons
　chopped shallot, divided

4 tablespoons vegetable oil, divided

6 medium-size tomatoes

½ pineapple, peeled, cored,
　and sliced

To garnish:

2 tablespoons chopped
　spring onions

2 tablespoons chopped fresh
　cilantro

Sweet and sour is a classic pairing in Vietnam and more widely in Asia. Use a good, heat-retaining pan so you can get your ribs succulent and sticky. The lemon and apple juices add a mild acidity, which helps the meat come off the bones.

To prepare the ribs: Place the water, salt, and sliced ginger in a large pot over high heat. Bring the water to a boil, add the ribs, and boil vigorously for 5 minutes. Lower the heat to medium and cook for another 10 minutes, or until the ribs are tender. Remove the ribs to a large dish and discard the cooking water. Pat the ribs dry with a paper towel.

In a small bowl, mix together the gia vi, fish sauce, lemon juice, apple juice, pepper, ½ tablespoon garlic, and 1 tablespoon shallot. Pour this mixture over the ribs, cover the dish, and let it stand at room temperature for 20 minutes.

Heat 3 tablespoons of the oil in a very large frying pan over medium-high heat, then add the remaining 2 tablespoons of garlic and toss until the oil is golden and fragrant (about 5 minutes). (You'll use this pan later to fry the ribs, which should fit in a single layer in the pan.) Carefully strain the garlic oil through a fine mesh sieve so you have just the oil without any pieces of garlic. Discard the garlic.

Pour the strained oil back into the frying pan over medium-high heat; add the ribs and fry until the ribs are golden, crispy, and fragrant from the oil: 5 to 7 minutes per side. Remove the ribs from the pan and set them aside. Wipe out the skillet to use in the next step.

To make the sauce: Chop the tomatoes in half and then cut each half into thirds.

In a large skillet over medium-high heat, add the remaining 1 tablespoon of oil and the remaining 2 teaspoons of chopped shallot and toss until the oil is fragrant. Then add the chopped tomatoes and sauté for 5 to 10 minutes until the tomatoes have softened. Taste the seasoning and adjust with more fish sauce or sugar if necessary.

Add the fried ribs, reduce the heat to low, and cover the pan. Cook for 45 minutes, or longer if you prefer your ribs softer. Ten minutes before serving, add the pineapple slices to the pan.

Garnish with the chopped spring onion and cilantro and serve with rice or noodles.

Temple Tofu

SERVES 4

For the tofu:
2 cups/500 ml water
1 tablespoon salt
1 tablespoon vinegar or lemon juice
18 ounces/500 g fresh firm tofu
1 cup/240 ml vegetable oil, divided

For the sauce:
6 tomatoes
1 tablespoon crushed garlic
2 tablespoons gia vi (or a mix
  of 2 parts sugar, 1 part sea salt,
  1 part ground black pepper,
  1 part garlic powder)
1 tablespoon granulated sugar
3 cups/750 ml water
2 lemongrass sticks, finely chopped
4 tablespoons soy sauce, divided

To serve:
2 tablespoons chopped cilantro

A few years ago we visited Phu Quoc, an island off the coast of Vietnam, for the first time. As we explored it we came across a temple. There was a feeling of stillness which drew us in, and, before we knew it, we'd walked right through to the back of the building where we found a kitchen. A young monk was making a fresh batch of tofu, churning the soy milk until it coagulated, like butter. A couple of nuns were cooking on wood-fired stoves, preparing a communal meal of curried tofu with coconut milk. The monk started chatting with us, and we didn't go anywhere else that day . . . or the next.

He showed us how to make soy milk, and explained how to make tofus of variable softness. With each meal, we discovered completely new ways of cooking vegan food: from tofu salads to fried tofu with lemongrass. The food was so light, it lifted our spirits and we felt completely energized by the time we finally left the temple.

To prepare the tofu: Combine the hot water, salt, and vinegar in a large pan over high heat, and bring the mixture to a boil. Add the tofu and boil for 5 to 7 minutes, then drain the tofu, and transfer it to a chopping board to cool. Drain and discard the cooking liquid.

When the tofu is cool, cut it into large thick slices and use a paper towel to pat it dry. It's important that the tofu is dry so that it will be nice and crispy later.

Measure out the 1 cup/240 ml of oil; pour two tablespoons of the oil into a small bowl and set aside. In a frying pan, heat the remaining oil over medium heat. When the oil is hot, add the tofu pieces in batches so they are submerged in the oil. When you see the bottom of the tofu turning yellow and crispy, after 1 to 3 minutes, turn it over so it cooks evenly.

Drain the fried tofu on a plate lined with a paper towel to soak up the excess oil.

To make the sauce: Chop the tomatoes into chunks (about 6 to 8 chunks per tomato).

(Recipe continues)

In a heavy-bottomed pan, heat the remaining 2 tablespoons of oil, then add the crushed garlic and toss for about 1 minute until fragrant. Add the chopped tomatoes and toss again for about 5 minutes. Add the gia vi and the sugar and cook for another 5 minutes over medium heat, until the tomatoes soften slightly. Pour in the water, add the lemongrass, and continue to cook for another 10 minutes, until the liquid is sauce-like.

Add the tofu to the pan, then stir in 2 tablespoons of the soy sauce and cook for another 10 minutes, until the tofu soaks up the flavors of the sauce. Now add the remaining soy sauce and turn the heat down to low. Continue to simmer the tofu for another 15 minutes.

Sprinkle with chopped cilantro and serve with steaming hot rice or noodles.

Shrimp Tamarind

SERVES 2

For the tamarind sauce:

2 tablespoons tamarind pulp,
  cut from a slab (see page 226)

4 tablespoons hot water,
  plus more as needed

2 tablespoons granulated sugar

2 tablespoons fish sauce

1 teaspoon finely chopped
  lemongrass

For the shrimp:

1 tablespoon vegetable oil

1 tablespoon crushed garlic

1 teaspoon chopped shallot

5 ounces/150 g fresh medium
  shrimp, peeled and deveined

To garnish:

2 spring onions, sliced

A few sprigs cilantro

This dish dates back to our first supper clubs. Once our stall was going strong on Broadway Market we began hosting pop-up supper clubs in local restaurants. These were great fun to cook for, as the guests would take pleasure in each dish as it appeared. This recipe shows how a good sauce can make a dish. With sauces, cooks can let their imagination run free, and Anh is always coming up with new concoctions.

To make the sauce: In a small bowl, soak the tamarind pulp in just enough hot water to cover it for 10 to 20 minutes, until it becomes soft. Using a fine-mesh sieve, strain the juice into a mixing bowl; discard the solids. Stir in the sugar, fish sauce, and lemongrass. (If you want a slightly sourer or sweeter sauce, adjust the quantities to your taste.)

To cook the shrimp: Heat the oil over medium-high heat in a frying pan or wok and sauté the crushed garlic and chopped shallot for a few minutes until fragrant. Stir in the shrimp, turning them frequently. When they start to turn pink, add the tamarind sauce and simmer for a couple of minutes to marry the flavors.

Garnish with slices of spring onion and sprigs of cilantro before serving.

Shrimp Tamarind, page 79

Festive Cooking
(An Qua)

Vegetables are plentiful in Vietnamese cooking, and fresh herbs accompany every dish. On any festive occasion, the table spread is verdant with fresh herbs and vegetable dishes. Surprisingly, strictly vegetarian dishes can be hard to find. We might make a simple fried tofu or a plate of steamed vegetables but then pair it with an exquisite chili-lime-fish sauce dipping sauce. It's unthinkable to omit fish sauce in Vietnam—like trying to cook Italian without olive oil. In Vietnam, much of vegetarian cooking stems from the Buddhist traditions, but even they seem to have overlooked the festive broths of communal dining.

So we set out to cook a really good vegetarian noodle soup. Browsing the neighboring vegetable market stall, we didn't need to look far, as any mixture of root vegetables— parsnips, celery root, rutabaga, carrots, or turnips—makes for a really good broth base (see page 211). Pair the sweetness of the root vegetables with a signature Vietnamese contrast of flavors—sourness from tamarind or tomatoes—then add some fresh herbs and a kick of chile, and you have an ingenious sweet and sour vegetable noodle soup.

■ ■ ■ ■

Sweet and Sour Tofu Noodle Soup

SERVES 2

1 generous quart/1 L vegetable broth
  (see page 211, or store-bought)
1 (14-ounce/400-g) pack bun
  rice noodles
3 medium-size tomatoes
½ cup/100 g pineapple chunks
7 ounces/200 g fresh firm tofu,
  diced
1 tablespoon soy sauce
1 tablespoon chopped spring onions
1 tablespoon chopped fresh cilantro

Here the sweet and sour complement each other, adding interest rather than taking anything away from the dish.

Bring the vegetable broth to a boil in a large pot over high heat. Cut the tomatoes in half, and then cut each half into thirds. Add the tomatoes, pineapple and tofu pieces to the broth and reduce to a simmer. Season with 1 tablespoon of soy sauce, or to taste.

Meanwhile, cook the noodles according to the packet instructions.

Divide the noodles between 2 bowls, and then pour the broth over them. Sprinkle with the chopped spring onions and cilantro, and serve.

Social Cooking

(An Choi)

A crisp, mild sourness, balanced out with sugar and spiced up with chiles, is a simple formula for failsafe salad dressings. Salads are some of the most little-known yet enjoyable Vietnamese dishes for Western tastes. We don't actually eat leaves raw—fresh herbs being an exception—so the vegetables are usually lightly pickled to infuse the flavors. Salads feature prominently on celebratory menus, and whether it's for a New Year's celebration or the christening of a child, their herb-filled lightness makes for a snacky respite amid an otherwise heavy meal.

■ ■ ■ ■

Papaya Salad with Crispy Anchovies

SERVES 4

1 green papaya
   (about 10 ounces/300 g)
1 carrot
1 teaspoon salt, plus more as needed
Vegetable oil for deep-frying
1 ounce/30 g dried anchovies
Pinch of granulated sugar
1 tablespoon chopped rau ram or
   cilantro, plus extra sprigs
   for garnishing
1 tablespoon chopped mint leaves,
   plus extra sprigs for garnishing
1 firm mango
Garlic, Lime, and Chile
   Dipping Sauce (page 218)
½ cup/100 g roasted salted
   peanuts, crushed

Anh's favorite streetside stall in Hanoi, next to a bustling market, served papaya salad. This salad usually comes with beef, shrimp, or even grilled quail. We tried several variations of our own before hitting on the idea of using deep-fried dried anchovies. The crisp texture of the anchovies contrasts beautifully with the papaya. This is delicious dressed with the Garlic, Lime, and Chile Dipping Sauce (page 218). Top with a sprinkling of fresh herbs and ground peanuts before serving.

Dried anchovies are available at most Asian supermarkets, and we use a quick frying technique to make them crispy again.

Peel the papaya and carrot. Rinse the papaya in cold water to remove the resin from the green fruit, then cut the fruit in half and remove the seeds. Shred the papaya and carrot into long slithers using a grater or food processor with the grating attachment.

Soak the shredded papaya and carrot in cold water with 1 teaspoon of salt for 10 minutes. Drain and leave the mixture to dry in a colander.

Fill a small, heavy-bottomed pan with 1 scant inch/2 cm of oil and heat over medium-high heat. To test if the oil is hot enough, drop in an anchovy; if it sizzles, the oil is ready. Deep-fry the anchovies, a few at a time, until slightly brown, and then carefully remove them to a plate lined with a paper towel to drain.

Tip the fried anchovies into a bowl. Sprinkle a pinch of sugar and salt over them and shake well.

In a separate large bowl, mix the shredded papaya and carrot with the chopped herbs. Peel and shred the mango and add it in. Dress the papaya with the Garlic, Lime, and Chile Sauce. Divide the salad among individual serving plates, and top with the anchovies and crushed peanuts. Garnish with a few extra sprigs of herbs.

Note: Green papaya is a special variety found in Asian supermarkets. You can substitute with kohlrabi or even green apples. But don't use yellow papaya as it will disintegrate.

Beef Carpaccio with Red Onion and Herb Salad

SERVES 4

11 ounces/300 g sirloin steak
2 medium-size red onions
1 generous quart/1 L hot water
Pickle Brine (page 213)
Juice of 3 limes, plus 4
    wedges for garnish
7 ounces/200 g bean sprouts
2 tablespoons chopped cilantro, plus
    a few sprigs for garnish
5 tablespoons Garlic, Lime, and
    Chile Dipping Sauce (page 218)
1 tablespoon crushed peanuts
2 red chiles, chopped

I didn't believe Anh when she first told me that we could "cold cook" meat. The first time she prepared this dish, I made her sear the beef again, almost turning it into a stir-fry. If you can slice the beef very thinly, it's best eaten raw—simply steeped in the lime and chiles. If you prefer your meat more rustic and thick-cut, flash-fry it for a moment before you add the dressing.

Cut the beef into very thin slices. This is easy to do if you part-freeze it first (page 231).

Cut the red onions into quarters, and then into thin slices. Place the onion slices in a medium bowl and pour the hot water over top. Let the onions steep for a couple of minutes before draining them.

Place the steeped onions in a sealed container or sterilized jar, and pour in enough pickle brine so that the onions are fully submerged. Cover the container or jar and let it sit at room temperature while you prepare the rest of the dish. They should still be crunchy, as they'll be used right away in the salad.

Place the juice from the limes into a bowl. Dip the thin slices of beef into the lime juice and swish each slice around for a few seconds. This will "cook" the beef. Even without heat, the beef should turn from the bright red color of raw meat to the light brown color of seared meat. Layer them over a large serving plate.

Drain the pickled onions, and scatter the onion slices over the plate of beef along with the bean sprouts and chopped cilantro.

Pour the Garlic, Lime, and Chile Dipping Sauce over the salad, and sprinkle the peanuts and chile over top. Garnish with sprigs of cilantro and the wedges of lime on the side.

Shredded Chicken, Red Onion, and Herb Salad

SERVES 4

2 medium-size red onions
1 generous quart/1 L hot water
Pickle Brine (page 213)
2 boneless, skinless chicken thighs
Pinch of salt
1 (2-inch/5-cm) piece fresh ginger, peeled and thinly sliced
5 tablespoons Garlic, Lime, and Chile Dipping Sauce (page 218)
1 tablespoon crushed peanuts
2 tablespoons chopped rau ram or cilantro, plus a few sprigs for garnish
3½ ounces/100 g shredded banana blossom (optional)

This shredded chicken salad is a taste of summer. The banana blossom is optional but it adds a wonderful earthy taste. Many parts of the banana tree are widely used in Vietnamese cooking. It's an example of Vietnamese resourcefulness, as the leaves are used to wrap around sticky rice or cover fish on the grill, the blossoms are made into salads, and even the porous banana trunk is sliced thinly to serve with fresh herbs.

Cut the red onions into quarters, and then into thin slices. Place the onion slices in a medium bowl and pour the hot water over top. Let the onions steep for a couple of minutes before draining them.

Place the steeped onions in a sealed container or sterilized jar, and pour in enough pickle brine so that the onions are fully submerged. Cover the container or jar and let it sit at room temperature while you prepare the rest of the dish. They should still be crunchy, as they'll be used right away in the salad.

In a small saucepan, combine the chicken thighs with a pinch of salt and the slices of fresh ginger. Cover with water and bring to a boil over high heat, then reduce the heat to low and simmer for about 25 minutes, or until the chicken is cooked.

Remove the chicken thighs from the cooking liquid and transfer them to a bowl of cold water to stop the cooking and cool them down. After a couple of minutes, drain the water and shred the chicken into thin strips.

In a serving bowl, mix together the red onions and shredded chicken. Pour the Garlic, Lime, and Chile Dipping Sauce over top and toss to combine. Sprinkle the peanuts, chopped herbs, and banana blossom over the salad, and garnish with a few extra sprigs of herbs before serving.

Note: The shredded banana blossom provides a crunchy texture and earthy flavor, and is available all year round in Asian supermarkets. You can also buy whole banana blossoms and serve individual portions of salad in these beautiful big red petals to wow your guests.

Red Cabbage and Bean Sprout Salad with Herbs

SERVES 4

½ medium-size red cabbage, cored
Hot water, as needed
2 teaspoons salt, divided
1 teaspoon granulated sugar
1 tablespoon vinegar, like rice
  vinegar or fruit vinegar
1 cup/100g beansprouts
1 bunch rau ram or mint,
  chopped

This very simple winter salad makes a sumptuous companion to stews and braised dishes. For instance, the sweetness of the Caramelized Braised Pork Belly recipe (page 31) cries out for the contrasting acidity of this salad. It also works well as a crispy snack with rice crackers. Rice vinegar and fruit vinegars such as cider vinegar are fine to use here, but avoid malt, wine, and balsamic vinegars as they are too acidic.

On a chopping board, hold the red cabbage firmly and use a sharp knife to grate off thin slivers.

Place the thinly sliced cabbage in a large bowl, cover it with hot water, and stir in 1 teaspoon of the salt; let the cabbage soak for 5 minutes. Drain and discard the soaking liquid, and place the cabbage in a colander to dry.

Once the cabbage is dry, place it in a large bowl and sprinkle with the remaining 1 teaspoon of salt and the sugar. Squeeze the cabbage with your hand so that the sugar and salt is absorbed into the cabbage.

Add the vinegar to the bowl, and use your hand again to squeeze the cabbage so the flavors are absorbed fully.

Add the bean sprouts and chopped rau ram or mint, and toss well before serving.

Scrambled Egg with Tomato and Spring Onion

SERVES 1

1 egg
½ teaspoon gia vi (or a mix
   of 2 parts sugar, 1 part sea salt,
   1 part ground black pepper,
   1 part garlic powder)
½ teaspoon fish sauce
1 medium-size tomato
1 tablespoon vegetable oil
1 tablespoon chopped
   spring onion

This is our emergency recipe, for when the fridge is empty but we are hungry and need a meal in 10 minutes. We dash to the corner shop for a carton of eggs, a couple of tomatoes, and a bunch of spring onions. This is simple to cook but delicious. It is also a great recipe for a weekend breakfast.

In a bowl, whisk the egg and season with the gia vi and fish sauce.

Cut the tomato in half and then cut each half into thirds.

Heat the oil in a small, heavy-bottomed pan over medium-high heat, then add the tomato and stir until soft, 3 to 5 minutes. Pour the egg mixture over the tomato, and cook over medium-low heat, stirring frequently, until the egg is fluffy but still moist, another 3 to 5 minutes, or until it is done to your liking.

Sprinkle with chopped spring onion and serve with rice or bread.

SPICINESS
&
ADVENTURE

Chapter 3

Many people assume that Vietnamese food is spicy, like Thai. But Vietnam is a long, thin country and its cooking varies hugely from one region to another. In the south and center, chiles are used liberally, but in the north, where we come from, strong spices are used sparingly. We favor subtle sweetness, which is why we Hanoians do the best pho.

Chiles are the loudest spice; they're small but attention-seeking. However, there are other spices which deserve more recognition than they get. Ginger brings a warm, fragrant spiciness to dishes; we often pair it with seafood because its elegant scent eliminates any fishy odor. Lemongrass, in marinades, stir-fries, and noodle soups, adds a subtly spicy heat. Black pepper is the most versatile spice, packed with aroma that transforms a dish.

It wasn't until we moved to New York that we really got into spicy food. We were both in our twenties, in our first jobs and truly independent for the first time in our lives. We lived in a fifth-floor walk-up apartment in Long Island City with a view of the Manhattan skyline across the bridge. On summer nights, we would pull up the window and sit on the fire escape with our feet dangling, mesmerized by the lights of that iconic skyline.

We spent that whole year eating. We tried the midtown lunch scene's chi-chi sandwiches, ate roasted chestnuts after skating in Bryant Park, nibbled seafood pancakes in late-night Korea Town, had tea on the Bergdorf Goodman store rooftop looking out toward Central Park, spun cotton candy at St Mark's Place, and picked Sunday dim sum from the steaming trolleys in Flushing.

Most exciting of all were Saturdays: We'd ride the N train to Canal Street on a pilgrimage to the famous Paris Deli, renowned for its Vietnamese banh mi. We'd order the Number 1 Special, together with a bubble tea, and stock up with three or four baguettes for the rest of the weekend.

Paris Deli epitomized the New York attitude toward food—it was less about taste and more about abundance. It was always open, always busy, and there were so many options to choose from! The banh mi of our childhood in Vietnam had just a smear of pâté, a little butter, scraps of roast pork, and some sprigs of cilantro. Now Paris Deli showed us that banh mi should come in a dozen flavors, from turkey and cheese to sardine. It must also be very spicy and served with a generous dollop of the great Vietnamese-American success story, Sriracha sauce, with the rooster on its bottle. This loud food was a far cry from what we grew up with in the isolated Vietnam of the 1980s.

I am grateful to Paris Deli, because without its massive store in Chinatown, the idea of banh mi as an urban food would never have captured my imagination. And I'm grateful we ended up coming to London, because in New York we might never have seen the world in daylight and got off the merry-go-round of consumption, to start being creative.

Everyday Cooking
(An Com)

After our last year at Oxford University, Anh and I went on a road trip in Tibet. We wanted to learn how spices like ginger and chiles were used in different ways in everyday cooking across Asia. To reach the Tibetan capital, Lhasa, we crossed the Himalayan mountain range, which was more spectacular than I could have imagined. We spiraled through mountain passes in heavy snow, which opened out onto immense spaces. We saw herds of antelope, and yaks herded by nomadic shepherds whose temporary huts were covered with prayer flags, and we passed pilgrims on foot coated in dust.

One night we stayed in a Tibetan home. I can't remember what it looked like, except that the bed was a concrete platform with an oven underneath and colorful flowery blankets on top. But we both clearly remember our breakfast the next morning. We were fed a potato noodle soup with a steamy vegetable broth, served in cast-iron pots. I noticed the slices of ginger floating around in the massive soup bowl and it struck me that even though we'd never had potato noodle soup before, all our lives we had slurped great-tasting broth fragrant with ginger. Ginger is the ideal ingredient for simple, everyday cooking. Unlike other spices, its heat is not burning, but comfortingly warm and cleansing.

■ ■ ■ ■

Watercress, Clam, and Ginger Soup

SERVES 4

11 ounces/300 g fresh clams,
   scrubbed clean
5 cups/1.2 L water
Pinch of salt
1 (2-inch/5-cm) piece fresh ginger,
   peeled and thinly sliced
2 teaspoons fish sauce
1 teaspoon gia vi (or a mix
   of 2 parts sugar, 1 part sea salt,
   1 part ground black pepper,
   1 part garlic powder)
1 bunch watercress, trimmed
   and chopped

Clams are possibly the easiest way to a great seafood broth. We use them to make broth for soups and hotpots. The warmth of ginger balances the seafood, which is considered a "cold" food: it's a bit of yin and yang.

Rinse the clams to remove any grit. In a large pan, bring the water to a boil with a pinch of salt. Add the clams and the sliced ginger and cook until the clams open, which means they are cooked.

Season with the fish sauce and gia vi and add the watercress a couple of minutes before serving. Discard any clams that don't open. Serve hot, with an empty bowl for the clam shells.

Spicy Root Vegetable Soup

SERVES 2

14 ounces/400 g celery root

11 ounces/300 g rutabaga

4 medium-size vine tomatoes

1 generous quart/1 L water

1 teaspoon gia vi (or a mix
   of 2 parts sugar, 1 part sea salt,
   1 part ground black pepper,
   1 part garlic powder)

1 teaspoon chopped small red chiles

7 ounces/200 g cubed
   pineapple

Winter root vegetables often seem so impenetrable with their thick skin and weight that we're tempted to leave them in the vegetable rack. We favor delicate leafy vegetables that demand we do something with them while their goodness lasts. Yet root vegetables are packed with flavor, and where we once might have used a couple of shrimp or a cup of chicken stock to cook leafy vegetables, now we often simply use the broth from celery root and rutabaga. They make the perfect vegetarian broth and here, where they offset the sweet tomato and the sour pineapple, their flavors hit just the right note.

Peel the celery root and rutabaga and cut them into 1½-inch/3-cm cubes. Chop the tomatoes in half, and then cut each half into thirds.

Bring the water to a boil in a large pan over high heat. Add the celery root and rutabaga, reduce the heat to medium, and simmer for 20 minutes, until soft. If you have more time, you can leave it to cook for longer over a low heat. Season with the gia vi and add the tomatoes and chile. Add the pineapple cubes, and cook for another 7 minutes. Serve hot.

Tofu with Lemongrass and Chile

SERVES 4

For the tofu:

2 cups/500 ml hot water

1 tablespoon salt

1 tablespoon vinegar or lemon juice

18 ounces/500 g fresh firm tofu

2 fresh lemongrass sticks,
    finely chopped

1 scant cup/200 ml vegetable oil

For the dipping sauce:

2 teaspoons soy sauce

½ teaspoon chopped fresh chiles,
    or to taste

At the island temple where we learned to cook Temple Tofu (page 76) we learned more ways to cook tofu than we had ever thought possible. This recipe is for a traditional fried tofu, but we have breaded it with chopped lemongrass to give it an extra dimension.

To prepare the tofu: Pour the hot water into a large pan set over high heat, add the salt and vinegar, and bring to a boil. Add the tofu and boil for 5 to 7 minutes, then drain the tofu, place it on a plate, and set it aside to cool at room temperature. This will revive the tofu and clean it of any sourness.

When the tofu is cool, cut it into large, thick slices and use a paper towel to pat it dry. It's very important that the tofu is dry so that it will be nice and crispy later.

Use a small sharp knife to make shallow slits in the tofu so the lemongrass will stick to it.

Spread the chopped lemongrass on a plate, and then coat the tofu with it, using your hands to rub it into the cuts that you made with the knife.

In a frying pan, heat the oil over medium heat. To test that the oil is hot enough, drop in a small piece of lemongrass. If it sizzles right away, the oil is ready. Add the tofu so that it's submerged in the oil. When you see the bottom of the tofu turning yellow and crispy, turn it over so it cooks evenly. Drain the finished tofu on paper towels.

To make the dipping sauce: Pour the soy sauce into a bowl and add as much chile as you are comfortable with. Serve the tofu hot, with the dipping sauce on the side.

Pan-Fried Pork Belly with Black Pepper and Spring Onion

SERVES 4

14 ounces/400 g lean pork belly

2 teaspoons freshly ground
   black pepper

1 teaspoon gia vi (or a mix
   of 2 parts sugar, 1 part sea salt,
   1 part ground black pepper,
   1 part garlic powder)

2 tablespoons fish sauce

2 teaspoons granulated sugar

2 teaspoons crushed garlic

2 teaspoons chopped shallot

2 tablespoons vegetable oil

2 bunches spring onions, finely
   chopped

Pork belly is one of the most versatile cuts of meat and can be cooked in a variety of ways. It can be steamed and used as a filling for summer rolls, or braised and eaten with rice. While our Caramelized Braised Pork Belly recipe (page 31) needs a slow simmer, this pan-fried pork belly recipe is quick, and the meat comes out crispy with honeyed edges.

Slice the pork belly thinly and place it in a shallow dish. In a small bowl, combine the pepper, gia vi, fish sauce, sugar, garlic, and shallot, and pour the mixture over the pork. Cover the dish and place it in the fridge for 15 to 25 minutes.

Heat the oil in a frying pan over medium-high heat. Stir in the pork belly and turn the heat down to medium-low. Cover with a lid and cook for about 7 minutes, until the meat is soft and moist. Remove the lid and toss the pork around vigorously until it's golden and crispy, another 7 to 9 minutes.

Scatter the chopped spring onions over the pork and stir for another 2 to 3 minutes, until the onion is just wilted and fragrant. Serve immediately.

Shaking Beef with Black Pepper

SERVES 4

1 pound/500 g sirloin steak

3 tablespoons vegetable oil, divided

1 teaspoon chopped garlic

½ teaspoon gia vi (or a mix
   of 2 parts sugar, 1 part sea salt,
   1 part ground black pepper,
   1 part garlic powder)

2 tablespoons soy sauce

2 tablespoons oyster sauce

2 tablespoons fresh pear juice

1 tablespoon fresh
   pineapple juice

1 tablespoon freshly ground black
   pepper, plus more to taste

1 teaspoon crushed garlic

To serve:

Butter lettuce or watercress

Sliced pineapple

Sliced cucumber

Cubed beef steak is a popular dish in Vietnam because it goes perfectly with a draught beer. This is why it often appears on the menus in Vietnam's many watering holes. Here is Banhmi11's twist on this recipe. We serve it with homemade chips and a watercress salad, and it has wowed many a dinner guest. It's extremely easy to cook, but, as with all steaks, make sure you ask your butcher for a nice, tender cut.

Cut the steak into bite-size cubes.

Combine 1 tablespoon of vegetable oil, the chopped garlic, gia vi, soy sauce, oyster sauce, pear juice, pineapple juice, and 1 tablespoons of pepper in a large dish. Add the beef cubes, turning to coat them in the marinade, and then cover the dish, and let the meat marinate at room temperature for up to 1 hour.

Heat the remaining 2 tablespoons of oil in a large wok over high heat. Add the crushed garlic and toss until the oil is fragrant, 1 minute.

Gradually add the marinated beef to the pan in small batches and toss for a couple of minutes, shaking the pan so the meat is evenly coated and removing the meat from the pan when it is browned on all sides, about 5 minutes per batch for medium-rare and 7 minutes for medium. Take care not to overcook it or it'll become very tough.

To serve, arrange the lettuce on serving plates with the pineapple and cucumber. Top with the beef and sprinkle with black pepper to taste.

Note: You can also thread the beef cubes onto skewers with sliced red or green peppers and then grill over charcoal for a tasty barbecue dish.

Wok-Fried Black Pepper Beef and Celery

SERVES 4

14 ounces/400 g sirloin steak

2 teaspoons freshly ground
  black pepper

1 teaspoon gia vi (or a mix
  of 2 parts sugar, 1 part sea salt,
  1 part ground black pepper,
  1 part garlic powder)

2 teaspoons granulated sugar

1 tablespoon crushed garlic, divided

2 teaspoons chopped shallot

6 celery stalks

4 tablespoons vegetable oil, divided

In Vietnam we like the soft texture of celery leaves more than the crunchy stalks, which we rarely eat. But this UK- and North America–friendly recipe uses the stalks. When you use a wok, the heat rises up the sides to maximize contact with the vegetables, plus the fragrance of caramelized garlic and onion is folded back into the food. If you don't have a wok, use a deep saucepan rather than a frying pan.

Slice the beef as thinly as you can and place the slices in a shallow dish.

In a small bowl, combine the pepper, gia vi, sugar, 2 teaspoons of the garlic, shallot, and 2 tablespoons of the oil and pour the mixture over the sliced beef, tossing to coat. Cover the dish and leave it in the fridge for 15 to 25 minutes.

Cut the celery into ½-inch/1-cm slices.

Heat the remaining oil in a wok or deep-sided, heavy-bottomed pan over medium-high heat. Add the remaining 1 teaspoon of garlic and stir vigorously until the oil is fragrant. Stir in the beef and flash-fry for 4 to 5 minutes. Add the sliced celery and continue to stir for a couple more minutes, depending on how you like your beef cooked. The celery should still be very crisp. Serve immediately.

Beef Stewed with Ginger

SERVES 4

1 tablespoon chopped garlic

½ teaspoon gia vi (or a mix
  of 2 parts sugar, 1 part sea salt,
  1 part ground black pepper,
  1 part garlic powder)

2 tablespoons soy sauce

2 tablespoons oyster sauce

2 tablespoons fresh pear juice

1 tablespoon fresh
  pineapple juice

1 tablespoon freshly ground
  black pepper

3 tablespoons vegetable oil, divided

1 pound/450 g diced stew beef

1 (2-inch/5-cm) piece fresh ginger,
  peeled and sliced

½ cup/120 ml water, or as needed

This beef stew is a hand-me-down from Anh's mother. It is a specialty of her hometown in central Vietnam. This dish is as comforting to us as Yorkshire pudding is to the British.

In a large bowl, combine the garlic, gia vi, soy sauce, oyster sauce, pear juice, pineapple juice, pepper, and 2 tablespoons of the oil. Add the beef, then cover the bowl and place it in the fridge for 20 minutes.

Heat the remaining tablespoon of oil in a flameproof casserole or large heavy-bottomed Dutch oven over high heat, and add the beef in its marinade and the ginger. Stir quickly, and then turn the heat down to low. Add ¼ cup/60 ml of the water and cover. Simmer over low heat. Check regularly and top up with ¼ cup/60 ml of water each time the meat begins to look dry. Cook for about 30 minutes total.

Serve with rice and braised greens.

French Beans with Garlic

This classic stir-fry with chopped garlic is for any meal and any time of the year.

SERVES 4

14 ounces/400 g French
   green beans
2 tablespoons vegetable oil
2 teaspoons crushed garlic
2 teaspoons fish sauce
2 teaspoons gia vi (or a mix
   of 2 parts sugar, 1 part sea salt,
   1 part ground black pepper,
   1 part garlic powder)

Break the beans into pieces about 2 inches/5 cm long.

Heat the oil in a wok or frying pan over high heat. Stir in the garlic and beans and cook for about 4 to 5 minutes, until the beans are cooked but still crunchy. Season with the fish sauce and gia vi and serve immediately.

Roast Chicken with Honey, Black Pepper, and Fish Sauce

SERVES 4

1 teaspoon crushed garlic

1 tablespoon fresh lemon juice

1 tablespoon fish sauce

1 teaspoon freshly ground
   black pepper

1 tablespoon honey

1 whole roasting chicken
   (about 3¼ to 3½ pounds/1.5 kg)

1 cup/240 ml water

Chicken holds a special place in Vietnamese food culture. It's often cooked on celebratory occasions. Before people sit down to eat, the chicken is offered to the spirits of the ancestors, and on New Year's Eve we eat chicken to give thanks for the past year.

This is our take on the Sunday roast. Here the chicken is basted in an intense, peppery honey marinade, which melds into the skin.

Combine the garlic, lemon juice, fish sauce, pepper, and honey in a small bowl.

Slit the skin of the chicken and rub the marinade under the skin, coating the chicken completely. Reserve any remaining marinade for basting the chicken later during cooking.

Set the chicken on a plate, cover with plastic wrap, and place it in the fridge for at least an hour.

Preheat the oven to 350°F/180°C/gas 4. When ready to cook, unwrap the chicken. Pour the water into a roasting pan and then place a roasting rack in the tray and sit the chicken on top. The water will produce steam to keep the chicken moist during cooking.

Roast the chicken in the oven for 1 hour and 20 minutes, or until the internal temperature reaches 180°F/82°C on an instant-read thermometer. Every 15 minutes or so, brush the chicken with the remaining marinade to keep it moist. To check if the chicken is cooked, insert a sharp knife or metal skewer into the thickest part of one of the thighs; if the juices run clear, the chicken is ready. If there are any pink juices, return the chicken to the oven for 10 to 15 minutes longer.

Serve with rice, a simple salad, or, best of all, just like a traditional Sunday roast with all the trimmings.

Clay Pot Chicken with Ginger

SERVES 4

1½ tablespoons crushed garlic, divided

2 tablespoons vegetable oil, divided

1 tablespoon chopped shallot

1 tablespoon granulated sugar

3 tablespoons fish sauce, plus more as needed

1 teaspoon gia vi (or a mix of 2 parts sugar, 1 part sea salt, 1 part ground black pepper, 1 part garlic powder)

1 tablespoon freshly ground black pepper

1 tablespoon thinly sliced kaffir lime leaves, plus 4 whole leaves for garnishing

11 ounces/300 g chicken thighs or drumsticks

1 generous inch/3 cm fresh ginger, peeled and thinly sliced

4 tablespoons water

There's a Vietnamese proverb that says chicken goes with kaffir lime leaves, and I'm not one to ignore age-old wisdom. Typically, this refers to a simple dish of steamed chicken that is neatly chopped and arranged on a plate with kaffir lime leaves spread on top. Here we've taken a classic braised dish—chicken with ginger—and adapted it by adding kaffir lime leaves. Our influence is the great many curries we've eaten since leaving Vietnam. The kaffir lime's coolness contrasts with the heat of the ginger, and lends a lush, tropical fragrance.

In a large bowl, combine 1 tablespoon garlic, 1 tablespoon vegetable oil, the shallot, sugar, fish sauce, gia vi, pepper, and sliced lime leaves. Add the chicken, turn to coat, then cover the bowl and let the chicken marinate in the fridge for up to 1 hour.

In a heavy-bottomed pan over medium heat, heat the remaining 1 tablespoon of oil with the remaining ½ tablespoon of crushed garlic and the ginger and toss for 2 to 3 minutes, until the oil is fragrant.

Add the chicken to the pan and toss for 2 to 3 minutes, then reduce the heat to low. Add the water and cook on low heat for around 45 minutes, until the chicken is tender with crispy skin and the sauce has thickened. Add a little extra fish sauce if you need to, depending on your taste.

Transfer the chicken to serving plates and garnish with the remaining whole kaffir lime leaves.

Note: Traditionally, this dish would be cooked in a clay pot rather than a pan, hence the name.

Salmon with Ginger Caramel

SERVES 4

For the marinade:

18 ounces/500 g salmon fillets

1 tablespoon fresh lemon juice

1 tablespoon gia vi (or a mix
   of 2 parts granulated sugar,
   1 part sea salt, 1 part ground black
   pepper, 1 part garlic powder)

1 tablespoon freshly ground
   black pepper

½ tablespoon loose green tea

2 tablespoons fish sauce

1 tablespoon granulated sugar

½ tablespoon crushed garlic

2 tablespoons chopped fresh ginger

1 tablespoon chopped
   galangal (or 1 extra tablespoon
   chopped ginger)

For the caramel sauce:

4 tablespoons granulated sugar

1 cup/240 ml water

2 inches/5 cm fresh ginger,
   peeled and thinly sliced

To cook the salmon:

1 tablespoon vegetable oil

7 ounces/200 ml coconut milk

2 bird's-eye chiles, finely chopped

This has to be our favorite way of cooking salmon. Fish is a staple food in Vietnam, especially in the Mekong Delta, where it's eaten every day. In my second year at university, I worked in the country-side of the Delta as a volunteer for a few weeks. The fish there are firm, white, and fatty, and they are simmered in caramel until tender and then spiced with chopped fresh chiles. Salmon is the ideal Western equivalent: flavorful and plump.

Cut the salmon fillets into 1½-inch/4-cm chunks. In a medium bowl, combine the lemon juice, gia vi, pepper, tea leaves, fish sauce, sugar, garlic, ginger, and galangal. Add the salmon to the bowl and rub the marinade into the salmon pieces. Cover the bowl and place it in the fridge for about 20 minutes.

To make the caramel sauce: Place a heavy-bottomed pan over medium heat, add the sugar, and heat for 2 to 3 minutes without stir-ring. Turn the heat down to low and stir constantly for about 2 to 3 minutes, until no grains of sugar are visible. The sugar will begin to melt and turn an amber brown color. Pay special attention to the color of the caramel under the bubbles, as it will darken very quickly. Add the water and cook until it boils. Don't worry if the sugar hardens upon contact with the water; it will melt as it cooks, forming a caramel sauce. Remove the pan from the heat.

Let the caramel sauce cool down for about 10 minutes at room temperature, and then stir in the sliced ginger.

Pour this sauce over the marinated salmon, then cover the bowl and return it to the fridge for another 20 minutes.

Now set a pan over medium heat and add the remaining tablespoon of vegetable oil. When the oil is hot, add the salmon and its marinade.

When the salmon starts to sizzle, pour in the coconut milk, and then taste the sauce again and add more fish sauce or sugar if nec-essary. Stir in the chopped chiles.

Turn the heat down to low and leave the salmon to simmer for about 25 minutes, until the salmon is cooked through and the sauce has thickened and reduced by half.

Serve with rice and pickles (page 213).

Festive Cooking
(An Qua)

Nowhere in Vietnam is the tradition of festive cooking taken as seriously as in the old imperial city of Hue. Nestled in central Vietnam, Hue has its own very distinctive "imperial" cuisine. Today, Hue has a feel of timeless tranquility, and we have more of a sense of belonging there than in Hanoi where we grew up. Just before we opened our market café, No.101, in Shoreditch, we took a trip back to Hue.

Appropriately, we ate like kings on that trip. We sat in restaurants that looked as if they hadn't changed in sixty years. And we sat in coffee shops, the only girls in a roomful of men with their newspapers and cigarettes. Everything tasted delicious—insanely delicious.

There is one particular meal from that trip that is etched on my mind: Hue's best-known specialty, spicy beef noodle soup, or *bun bo Hue*. Through coffee-shop chat, we heard that the city's best spicy soup was made by an old lady on the patio of a nearby house. She'd been serving soup there since before 1975; the feeling was that her soup was "true," unaffected by the vagaries of modem living. We were told we must go there at precisely 3 o'clock.

We arrived at the patio at quarter to three. There was nobody around except an old man arranging chairs, and we wondered if we'd come to the right place. We sat down at a small table. At a minute to three, three women ritualistically carried in two large stockpots of broth. One of the women, whom we guessed to be the maestro, took center stage and sat down.

The old man took our orders and both Anh and I chose a bowl *day du*, or "with everything," which is usually the most expensive dish on the nonwritten menu, with all of the house specialties.

Our bowls arrived full to the brim and steaming hot, fragrant with chile and lemongrass, and layered with thin slivers of beef. It was one of the spiciest broths I've ever eaten, not because of the floating chile oil so commonly used elsewhere, but because of the sparkling spiciness of slow-simmered lemongrass. We looked at each other and knew we were right to travel half the world to eat this soup. We finished our bowls and, even though we were full, ordered a third bowl to share. By the time we left the patio was packed with people, from families with young children to elderly people travelling from outside the city just for a bowl.

That little old lady was cooking something that appears on the menu of every Vietnamese restaurant in the world. She has been single-mindedly cooking the same dish for forty years, and she executes it with absolute flair. Back in London, the memory of that patio reassured me that something as makeshift as a market stall could be nurtured into an institution. If we, like the old lady, could cook simply and consistently, we might just have a chance.

■ ■ ■ ■

Imperial Spicy Beef and Lemongrass Noodle Soup (*Bun Bo Hue*)

SERVES 4

For the marinated beef:

18 ounces/500 g sirloin steak

1 teaspoon gia vi (or a mix
   of 2 parts sugar, 1 part sea salt,
   1 part ground black pepper,
   1 part garlic powder)

2 teaspoons fish sauce

1 (2-inch/5-cm) piece fresh
   ginger, peeled and grated or thinly
   sliced

For the broth:

2 quarts/2 L beef broth
   (see page 210, or store-bought)

3 tablespoons gia vi (or a mix
   of 2 parts sugar, 1 part sea salt,
   1 part ground black pepper,
   1 part garlic powder)

5 tablespoons fish sauce

1 bunch fresh lemongrass, crushed

1 large red onion, chopped

2 tablespoons diluted shrimp paste
   (page 231)

For the chile oil:

¼ cup/50 ml annatto seed oil
   (page 209) or vegetable oil

2 tablespoons dried chile flakes

5 fresh bird's-eye chiles, chopped

If simple, clear *pho* is the signature food of the restrained north, then spicy *bun bo Hue* is the signature food of central Vietnam. The first time Anh and I ate it was when we lived in New York in our early twenties. Our northern palate wasn't accustomed to the spiciness and we struggled, with tears in our eyes, to finish our bowls. But we sought it out again time after time until we could make our own.

To prepare the marinated beef: Slice the beef sirloin very thinly. Combine the marinade ingredients in a large bowl. Add the beef slices to the bowl, toss to coat them in the marinade, then cover the bowl and place it in the fridge for about 20 minutes.

To make the broth: Bring the beef broth to a boil in a large pan or stockpot over high heat. Stir in the gia vi and fish sauce, reduce the heat to medium-low, and continue to simmer while you add the lemongrass and the onion to the pan. Add hot water as needed to keep the broth topped up to the same level as when you started. (Do not add cold water as it will make the broth very cloudy.) Add the diluted shrimp paste to your broth a couple of teaspoons at a time over the next 20 minutes.

To make the chile oil: Heat the annatto seed or vegetable oil in a heavy-bottomed pan over medium-high heat, then add the dried chile flakes and chopped fresh chiles and toss for about 5 minutes, or until the chiles completely dissolve into the oil.

Add a couple of tablespoons of this chile oil to the broth, or to taste. You don't want the chile oil to overpower the sweetness of the broth. Taste the broth and adjust the seasoning if necessary.

To serve:

2 (14-ounce/400 g) packs rice
vermicelli noodles

To garnish:

Bean sprouts

Basil leaves

Butter lettuce leaves, torn

Lemon wedges

Fresh chiles, finely chopped

Shredded morning glory and banana
blossoms (optional)

To serve: Cook the noodles according to the packet instructions and divide them among your bowls. Arrange the uncooked marinated beef on top of the noodles. Bring the broth to a bubbling boil and ladle it into each bowl, distributing it evenly and stirring gently to cook the beef. Arrange the garnishes on separate plates and serve alongside the bun bo Hue bowls.

Note: When you add the fish sauce and the diluted shrimp paste to the broth, pour a small quantity into a ladle and slowly dip the ladle in the broth in a circular motion until the ladle is fully submerged. This ensures that the pungent smell disperses and doesn't overwhelm the dish.

The original bun bo Hue recipe uses a broth from beef bones as well as pig's trotter and pork hock. This makes the broth very rich, like Japanese ramen broth.

Imperial Spicy Beef and Lemongrass Noodle Soup
(Bun Bo Hue), page 122

Spicy Noodle Soup with Crabmeat and Shrimp
(Banh Canh Cua), page 126

Spicy Noodle Soup with Crabmeat and Shrimp (*Banh Canh Cua*)

SERVES 4

For the crabmeat and shrimp:

18 ounces/500 g fresh medium
   shrimp, unpeeled
2 quarts/2 L vegetable broth
   (see page 211, or store-bought)
1 tablespoon vegetable oil
1 shallot, finely chopped
10 ounces/300 g white crabmeat

For the chile saté:

3 fresh bird's-eye chiles
½ tablespoon salt
1 tablespoon fresh lemon juice
½ tablespoon thick (undiluted)
   shrimp paste

Of all the spicy food we ate in New York, our favorite was from a hole-in-the-wall restaurant we stumbled upon. We were driving through outer Queens, lost and hungry, when we spotted a small neon sign that read "Little Saigon."

We had no expectations. There was an old lady watching TV and a poster signed by the cast of *Cats* on the wall. We ordered the banh canh cua, a noodle soup with a red bisque-like broth made with chopped shrimp and crabmeat. When it arrived, we gasped at the attention to detail. It tasted spicy but so sweet, like summer heat offset by monsoon rain.

We ate at Little Saigon every Sunday for the rest of that year. After a while the old lady began sharing her recipes for home-made yogurt and mayonnaise for banh mi. She'd left Vietnam on a boat for Hong Kong and lived in a camp with three of her ten children for a few years. There she made yogurt and traded it for other foods. When she came to New York she helped set up Paris Deli and had written their original banh mi recipes. We were struck with awe.

After we left New York, we visited Little Saigon whenever we returned on business. On our last visit she told us she was moving back to Saigon to live with her children. We've never ordered banh canh cua at a restaurant since. Instead we decided to make it ourselves as a tribute to Little Saigon.

Peel the shrimp and keep the shells for the broth. Chop the shrimp into small pieces.

Bring the vegetable broth to a boil in a large pan or stockpot over high heat. Add the prawn shells, reduce the heat to low, and leave it to simmer, skimming off any foam that appears, while you make the rest of the soup.

Heat the vegetable oil in a small frying pan and add the chopped shallot. Sauté for a minute until the oil is fragrant. Stir in the chopped shrimp and the crabmeat and fry quickly. Remove to a plate and set aside.

For the broth seasoning:

2 tablespoons diluted shrimp paste
  (page 231)
2 tablespoons gia vi (or a mix
  of 2 parts sugar, 1 part sea salt,
  1 part ground black pepper,
  1 part garlic powder)
2 tablespoons fish sauce
½ tablespoon granulated sugar
2 tablespoons annatto seed oil
  (page 209) (optional)
1 tablespoon corn flour
4 tablespoons water

**To assemble the ban canh
cua bowls:**

9 ounces/250 g udon noodles
1 bunch spring onions, chopped
1 bunch cilantro, chopped
1 small bunch rau ram or mint,
  chopped

To make the chile saté: In a steamer (or a metal colander or steamer basket set over a pan of simmering water), lightly steam the chiles so they are soft but not overcooked, 5 to 7 minutes. Remove the chiles from the pot and chop them finely. In a medium bowl, combine the chiles with the salt, lemon juice, and thick shrimp paste.

To season the broth: Add the diluted shrimp paste to the simmering broth. Stir in the gia vi, fish sauce, and sugar. Then add the annatto seed oil (if using), followed by the chile saté.

In a small bowl, dissolve the corn flour in the water and pour the mixture into the broth, stirring to thicken it. The broth should become quite thick, like a soup, but not as thick as a sauce.

To assemble the banh canh cua bowls: Cook the noodles according to the packet instructions and divide them among your bowls. Arrange the prawns and crabmeat on top of the noodles. Sprinkle the spring onions, cilantro, and rau ram or mint over the seafood.

Strain the broth through a fine-mesh sieve into another large pot, discarding any solids. Bring the strained broth to a bubbling boil before ladling it into each bowl, distributing it evenly.

Note: The traditional recipe from Hue uses pork bones for the broth, but for our vegetable-based alternative you can use almost any root vegetable.

Social Cooking

(An Choi)

If pubs are the heart of British social life, then in Vietnam the bars selling fresh draught beer, *bia hoi*, are where friendships are made, deals struck, and secrets shared. The accompanying bar snacks, known as *nhau*, are the perfect pep-up on a long evening's drinking. Unusually for a girl, Anh grew up knowing this food from an early age.

Anh is the fourth daughter in a family of girls. After giving birth to three daughters in succession, when Anh's mother fell pregnant again she was convinced she was going to have a boy. She told her husband, who was stationed in Laos with the Army, to come home for the birth of his first son. When another girl was born, he just packed his bags and returned to duty, refusing to see her or give her a name. Anh's name, literally meaning "big brother," was given to her by a family friend.

But like most fathers, Anh's had his own way of doting on her: his was to train her in sports. Every week he would take her to the Army Club's swimming pool. While she did laps, he would wait patiently for her at the bia hoi across the road where, with a cold beer in hand, he would munch on roasted peanuts and a bowl of fresh chiles.

Back then, nhau bar snacks were very simple. In modern Vietnam, they now come in every conceivable flavor, from lobster to hog roast.

■ ■ ■ ■

Clams with Fresh Chiles and Lemongrass

SERVES 4

2 pounds/1 kg clams
1 cup/240 ml white wine
2 lemongrass sticks, chopped
2 fresh chiles, chopped

To garnish:
4 to 6 sprigs cilantro
2 to 3 sprigs rau ram or mint

Moules marinieres, Vietnamese-style. These are perfect with crispy, thin-cut French fries.

Soak the clams in a large bowl of cold water about 15 minutes before you want to cook them, to remove any sand or grit. Rinse well under cold running water.

Put the clams in a heatproof dish that will fit inside your wok or cooking pot. Pour the wine over them, and add the lemongrass and chiles.

Place the dish in the wok or cooking pot and pour enough water into the wok or cooking pot to come halfway up the sides of the dish.

Place the wok or pot over medium heat, cover, and bring the water to a boil. Cook the clams for about 15 minutes.

Carefully remove the dish from the pot. Transfer the clams to a serving dish, discarding any that aren't open. Garnish with sprigs of cilantro and rau ram.

Note: You can use pretty much any type of clams or mussels with this recipe.

Chargrilled Rice Paper with Quail Egg, Spring Onion, and Chile Flakes

MAKES 4

2 dozen small dehydrated shrimp
  (optional)
4 sheets rice paper
4 quail eggs
1 bunch spring onions, chopped
Dried chile flakes, to taste

In Vietnam the street-food stalls are huddled together. A drinks stall will set up next to a snacks stall, so customers can patronize both. Opposite the cathedral in Saigon, there's a small coffee place we love. One day we saw this curious dish being made at a makeshift stall nearby. That stall had the smallest footprint I had ever seen: the wife cooked from a small basket while the husband took the orders and the payment.

This is a quick and easy way to transform the rice paper commonly used for spring and summer rolls. Street-food ingenuity at its best!

If you are outdoors, use a charcoal grill or gas barbecue on a low flame. You can also cook this on a gas stove, using tongs to hold the rice paper about 6 inches/15 cm above the flame.

If using the shrimp, soak them for 10 minutes in hot water, then rinse and dry with a paper towel.

Using one sheet of rice paper at a time, roast it over a low flame for a couple of minutes, flipping it over frequently so the heat is evenly distributed.

Crack a quail egg on top and use a pastry brush in a circular motion to disperse the egg into a thin layer of omelet. Sprinkle with a few shrimp and some chopped spring onion and chile flakes. Take it off the grill when the rice paper is crispy and golden brown. Break it into slices and eat it as you would a pizza.

Repeat with the remaining sheets and eggs.

Hot Ginger Tea

MAKES 1 SCANT CUP/240 ML

½ cup/100 g granulated sugar

1 cup/240 ml hot water

7 ounces/200 g fresh ginger, peeled and finely chopped

Black or green tea leaves, as needed

This is a favorite on our winter drinks menu. The comforting heat from this ginger tea has cured many colds and coughs, while the syrup's sweetness is just what we crave as we await the arrival of spring.

In a heavy-bottomed pan, melt the sugar over medium-high heat. Stir with a wooden spoon so the sugar doesn't burn.

Once the sugar is amber brown and caramelized, pour in the hot water and cook for another 5 minutes, being sure to re-melt any sugar that seizes upon contact with the water.

In a separate frying pan, sauté the ginger over medium-low heat for 5 minutes until fragrant. Use a wooden spoon or chopsticks to toss the ginger so it doesn't burn. Then pour the sautéed ginger into the caramel water and simmer over low heat for 15 minutes.

Remove the pan from the heat and let the ginger syrup cool to room temperature, then pour it into a sterilized jar. It will keep, covered and refrigerated, for up to 2 weeks.

To make hot ginger tea: Brew a pot of strong black tea or roasted green tea.

To each cup add 2 tablespoons of ginger syrup, then pour the hot tea over the syrup.

Stir well and serve.

Note: To sterilize jars, wash them thoroughly in warm soapy water, then rinse them in clean warm water. Allow them to drip-dry, upside down, on a rack in a medium oven for 5 minutes.

BITTERNESS
&
PERSPECTIVE

Chapter 4

Bitterness is a flavor of perspective. It's subjective, in that a strong espresso may be unbearably bitter for one person but full of depth for another. Likewise, celery and leek have bitter notes for the Vietnamese palate, whereas in Europe they provide the sweet base for a ragù or vegetable soup.

Our perspective changes as we grow up and develop more esoteric tastes. Coffee, dark chocolate, and draught beer have incredible flavors, but they suit more mature taste buds than the sweet treats of childhood.

In our everyday lives, too, bitterness has its downsides and its rewards. Growing a small business is a nerve-wracking experience—when the food gets burnt, staff members leave, equipment fails, or bills stack up. Or when all these disasters come at once, like that first winter after we'd just opened our market cafe at 101 Great Eastern Street, and I wondered if I'd been right to talk Anh out of her secure city job to follow this dream.

To get this bitterness into perspective, I thought about the first time I learned to cope with bitter loss. It was when I returned to Vietnam for my mother's funeral, less than six months after the phone call that informed me she had been diagnosed with cancer. After completing the funeral rituals, my sister, my father, and I went on our first family holiday in ten years to a small coastal town in Central Vietnam. For our first meal, I took them to a fantastic restaurant I'd discovered on an earlier holiday. I'd always imagined taking my mother, after she'd recovered, to eat in this place. It seemed impossible that it was just the three of us sitting there eating the house noodle soup. As I sipped the thick broth I let the flavors absorb me and my mind go quiet. A love of food had been my mother's gift to me.

Back in London, I decided to quit my job and work at Banhmi11 full-time. I knew it would take time to grow the business, but I felt that good would come of it. Day-to-day worries would always crop up, but they would pass, too. As Anh and I said to each other, we just have to cook one dish right, make one person happy, and it all starts to make sense.

Everyday Cooking
(An Com)

Cooking would be so easy if it were soothing all the time. But the truth is, cooking is tiring. It requires strong hands and stamina. Failures are exasperating, like the week we went through twenty-three permutations of homemade pâté before we nailed the perfect texture. And sometimes they are terrifying, like when we turned off the wrong stove and burned the chicken the night before market day. It's difficult to cook a good meal when you are tired, fed up, or bored, and yet the same meal seems simple when you are untroubled.

So the reason we cook, apart from providing fuel for our bodies, is because we care. Our mothers sometimes complained, yet every day they cooked a new meal as elaborate as the last, in solitary silence under a spinning fan. It's not just about enjoyment in the kitchen, it's about what happens when we sit down together and share a meal. And this is never truer than when it comes to everyday cooking.

■ ■ ■ ■

Spinach and White Crabmeat Soup

SERVES 4

3⅓ cups/800 ml water

7 ounces/200 g fresh white
  crabmeat

19 ounces/500 g baby spinach

2 teaspoons fish sauce

2 teaspoons gia vi (or a mix
  of 2 parts sugar, 1 part sea salt,
  1 part ground black pepper,
  1 part garlic powder)

The mild bitterness of spinach combines with the sweetness of white crabmeat in this simple soup, which cooks in minutes and tastes scrumptious.

Bring the water to a boil in a medium saucepan over high heat, add the crabmeat, and reduce the heat to a simmer. Cook for 10 minutes, until the broth is sweet. Add the spinach and bring to a boil again, just long enough to wilt the spinach.

Season with the fish sauce and gia vi, and serve.

Eggs with Chives

SERVES 1

1 egg
½ teaspoon gia vi (or a mix
  of 2 parts sugar, 1 part sea salt,
  1 part ground black pepper,
  1 part garlic powder)
½ teaspoon fish sauce
1 tablespoon chopped chives
1 tablespoon vegetable oil

This recipe is for those days when you have to cook, but don't want to make an effort. It's super-quick to prepare. The egg's sweetness balances the bitterness of the chives, which, according to Chinese medicine, have a cooling effect on the body and fight fatigue.

In a bowl, whisk the egg and season with the gia vi and fish sauce. Stir in the chopped chives.

Heat the oil in a small frying pan over medium-low heat. Pour the egg mixture into the pan and cook, stirring frequently, until the egg is fluffy but still moist.

Serve with rice or toasted bread.

Shrimp and Pork with Bitter Melon

SERVES 4

3 dried wood ear mushrooms

5 dried shiitake mushrooms

2 ounces/50 g fresh peeled shrimp

3½ ounces/100 g ground pork

1 tablespoon fish sauce

½ tablespoon gia vi (or a mix
  of 2 parts sugar, 1 part sea salt,
  1 part ground black pepper,
  1 part garlic powder)

½ tablespoon granulated sugar

2 tablespoons chopped spring onion

1 shallot, chopped

2 bitter melons

The Vietnamese name for bitter melon, *kho qua*, translates as "suffering has passed." In Vietnam it is served as a reminder of tough times, and as an encouragement that they, too, will pass.

Place the wood ear and shiitake mushrooms in a medium bowl and cover them with hot water. After about 15 minutes, when the mushrooms have expanded, drain and rinse them under cold water; then pat them dry with a paper towel. Chop the mushrooms coarsely.

Chop the shrimp coarsely.

In a medium bowl, mix together the shrimp, ground pork, mushrooms, fish sauce, gia vi, sugar, spring onion, and shallot.

Place the bitter melons in a large bowl and pour very hot water over them to cover. Let them soak for 1 minute. This will make them slightly less bitter and they will turn a deep green color.

Cut the melons into round slices about 1 generous inch/3 cm thick. Use a spoon or small knife to scoop out the seeds. Now fill the melon rings with the pork and prawn mixture.

Place the filled melon rings in a single layer in a heatproof dish that will fit inside your wok or cooking pot. Place the dish in the pot and pour enough water into the pot to come halfway up the sides of the dish. Cover and place the pot over medium heat. Bring the water to a boil and cook the melons for 20 minutes, or until the filling is cooked through.

Serve with rice and vegetables, or a salad.

Note: Bitter melon, or bitter gourd, is like a squash but with a distinctive flavor. You can buy it in Asian or Caribbean supermarkets.

Zucchini and Seared Sirloin

SERVES 4

4 medium-size zucchini
18 ounces/500 g sirloin steak

For the dressing:
4 tablespoons granulated sugar
8 tablespoons water
8 tablespoons soy sauce
2 teaspoons grated fresh ginger
2 tablespoons sesame oil
2 clementines

To garnish:
2 tablespoons chopped
   fresh cilantro
2 teaspoons white sesame seeds
2 tablespoons dried shallot
   (or toasted dried onion)

The zucchini's edge of bitterness is preserved in this recipe by keeping it raw and real.

Cut the zucchini in half lengthways and use a vegetable peeler to shave off long, thin slices. They should look like very wide, flat noodles.

To make the dressing: Put the sugar and water in a medium saucepan over medium heat and bring to a simmer. When the sugar has completely dissolved, add the soy sauce, ginger, and sesame oil, and remove the pan from the heat. Cut the clementines in half and squeeze the juice into the pan. Whisk to combine, then pour the dressing into a large bowl.

Soak the zucchini slices in the dressing for 3 to 5 minutes, and then transfer them to a plate with a slotted spoon, reserving the dressing.

Cut the sirloin steak into thin slices, and marinate it in the remaining dressing for 15 minutes.

Set a frying pan or a griddle over high heat, and then lightly sear the sirloin slices on both sides, about 2 to 3 minutes per side.

Divide the sirloin slices between 4 serving plates.

Roll up the zucchini slices and arrange them alongside the seared sirloin on the individual plates.

Sprinkle the chopped cilantro, white sesame seeds, and shallot over the beef and serve.

Squid, Leek, and Pineapple Stir-Fry

SERVES 4

2 leeks
1 pineapple, peeled, quartered, and cored
2 tablespoons vegetable oil
2 teaspoons chopped garlic
14 ounces/400 g cleaned squid, cut into rings
2 tablespoons fish sauce

This is perhaps one of the more unusual combinations for the Western palate. But it works beautifully. The sweetness of the pineapple, the bitterness of the leek, and the crunchy elasticity of the squid are delicious together.

Cut the leeks in half lengthways and then chop them into 1- to 2-inch/3- to 5-cm chunks. Rinse them in a bowl of cold water to remove all the grit; change the water until it runs clean.

Cut the pineapple into slices about 1 scant inch/2 cm thick.

Heat the oil in a wok or frying pan over medium-high heat. Add the garlic and stir until the oil is fragrant and the garlic is lightly browned. Stir in the chunks of leek and cook until the leeks are just a little crunchy in the centers, and still very green.

Stir in the squid and season with the fish sauce. Cook for 2 to 3 minutes, until the squid starts to turn opaque. Finally, stir in the pineapple slices and cook for a couple of minutes over high heat: the pineapple should soften slightly, but still be crisp in the center.

Remove the pan from the heat and serve immediately.

Note: Take care not to overcook the squid or it will become tough and rubbery.

Stewed Chicken with Dates and Goji Berries

SERVES 4

For the chicken:

1 whole chicken, about 3¼ to 3½
   pounds/1.5 kg
1 tablespoon chopped fresh ginger
2 tablespoons vodka
1 tablespoon salt

For the stuffing:

6 dates
1 teaspoon goji berries
12 lotus seeds (optional)
12 dried longan fruit (optional)

For the marinade:

3 tablespoons fish sauce
½ tablespoon granulated sugar
1 tablespoon gia vi (or a mix
   of 2 parts sugar, 1 part sea salt,
   1 part ground black pepper,
   1 part garlic powder)
½ tablespoon lemon juice
2 cups/500 ml water

When my mother was in the hospital, we used to make her stew with goji berries. Goji berries, which are used in traditional Chinese medicine, can be found in health food shops. In this recipe, the sweetness of the broth masks the bitterness of the herbs.

At one of our favorite street food stalls in Hanoi, a woman stews chicken in cut-up soft drink cans. I find it amusing that such an important and ceremonial dish, one considered so curative, can be prepared in recycled soft drink cans: another example of Vietnamese resourcefulness.

Preheat the oven to 350°F/180°C/gas 4.

To prepare the chicken: Wash the chicken under cold running water. In a small bowl, combine the chopped ginger, vodka, and salt, and rub the mixture all over the chicken to clean and prepare the skin. Rinse carefully.

Place the chicken in a roasting pan. Roast the chicken in the oven for 5 to 10 minutes, just to dry the skin. When it no longer looks wet, remove it from the oven.

Stuff the chicken's cavity with the dates, goji berries, and the lotus seeds and longan fruit if you can find them.

Put the chicken in a large, heavy-bottomed saucepan. If you don't have a big enough pan, you can chop the chicken in half and put the stuffing on top.

In a small bowl, combine the fish sauce, sugar, gia vi, lemon juice, and water, and pour the mixture over the chicken. Cover the pan and cook over low heat for 1 hour and 15 minutes.

Make sure the chicken is thoroughly cooked before serving. Test by inserting a metal skewer or sharp knife into the thigh joint; if the juices run clear, the chicken is ready. If there are any pink juices, cook the chicken for another 10 to 15 minutes.

This recipe is perfect served with rice for a restorative dinner whenever you feel run down.

Sea Bass Steamed with Beer

SERVES 4

For the marinade:

1 tablespoon chopped fresh ginger

½ tablespoon crushed garlic

½ tablespoon freshly ground black pepper

½ tablespoon finely chopped lemongrass

1 teaspoon granulated sugar

2 tablespoons fish sauce

For the fish:

4 sea bass fillets, skin-on, about 2¼ pounds/1 kg in total

2 lemongrass sticks

1 bunch dill

3 ounces/100 ml dark beer

The Vietnamese have a special way of steaming fish so that it's packed with flavor. This is achieved primarily through the marinade, but also by replacing water with beer, so the fish benefits from the fermented flavor.

To make the marinade: In a large bowl, mix together the ginger, garlic, black pepper, lemongrass, sugar, and fish sauce. Set the marinade aside.

To prepare the fish: You can either cut the fish fillets into chunks or leave them whole; if you choose to leave them whole, slit the skin in 3 or 4 places.

Add the fish to the bowl with the marinade, rub the marinade into the fish, and let it sit at room temperature for 15 to 25 minutes.

Crush the lemongrass sticks with a rolling pin or the broad side of a knife. Stuff the fish with the dill (save a couple of sprigs for the garnish) and crushed lemongrass.

Put the beer in the bottom of a steamer and place the fish in a heatproof bowl above the beer. Steam the fish for about 10 to 15 minutes. (If you don't have a steamer; put the beer in a pan and the fish in a heatproof bowl, then place the bowl in a steamer basket or metal colander set above the pan.) About 5 minutes before the fish is ready (the flesh will turn from transparent pink to white), sprinkle a pinch of chopped dill on top.

This fish is great served with a summer salad.

Braised Eggplant

SERVES 4

2 small Japanese eggplants
6 medium-size tomatoes
2 tablespoons vegetable oil
2 teaspoons chopped shallot
4 tablespoons soy sauce
2 tablespoons gia vi (or a mix
   of 2 parts sugar, 1 part sea salt,
   1 part ground black pepper,
   1 part garlic powder)
1¼ cup/200 ml hot water
14 ounces/400 g firm tofu
2 tablespoons chopped fresh
   cilantro
Shiso leaves (optional),
   for serving

I can never resist plush, purple eggplants and always pick up a couple when I see them. I prefer smaller eggplants to the large, spongy types. Our mothers cooked eggplants with tofu, green plantains, and shiso. This is Anh's take on the traditional recipe, so beloved in the repertoire of everyday Vietnamese cooking.

Cut the eggplant in half lengthways and then cut it into slices about 1 scant inch/2 cm thick.

Cut the tomatoes in half and slice each half into 3 pieces.

In a heavy-bottomed braising pan or Dutch oven, heat the oil over medium heat and cook the shallot until the oil is fragrant and the shallot is slightly browned. Add the tomatoes and stir frequently so they don't stick to the bottom of the pan. Season with the soy sauce and gia vi.

Add the eggplant, followed by the hot water, then turn the heat to low and simmer for 20 to 30 minutes until the eggplant is soft.

Cut the tofu into 1-inch/3-cm cubes and add them to the pan about 10 minutes before serving. Continue cooking until the tofu has soaked up the flavors of the sauce.

Sprinkle with the chopped cilantro and shiso if you have some.

Note: Firm tofu is easier to handle, though soft tofu will work fine in this recipe.

Festive Cooking

(An Qua)

Sometimes the occasions for which we gather together are not to celebrate, to be happy, or to be cheerful, but rather to mourn, to lament, to grieve. I can count fewer than a handful of people with whom I could share a meal in times of sorrow, yet they are even more precious to me than those with whom I can easily share moments of joy.

On the day that my mother passed away, I arrived home after 24 hours of driving nonstop from London to Germany, and my aunt had cooked a feast of the magnitude of the New Year's dinner—seven courses with crispy golden spring rolls with crab and shrimp, vegetable soups, sticky rice with mung bean, chicken and lime leaf, glass noodle stir-fry. We ate solemnly in silence, but I have never felt a stronger bond with my kinfolk than during that dinner. When life tastes bitter, perhaps the best antidote is festivity.

■ ■ ■ ■

Duck Noodle Soup with Bamboo

SERVES 6

For the duck:

1 (5- to 5½-pound/2.5-kg) whole
   duck
Salt, as needed
1 tablespoon gia vi (or a mix
   of 2 parts sugar, 1 part sea salt,
   1 part ground black pepper,
   1 part garlic powder)
½ tablespoon freshly ground black
   pepper
½ tablespoon finely chopped fresh
   ginger
½ tablespoon crushed garlic
8 generous cups/2 L hot water

To season the broth:

1 large onion, unpeeled
11 ounces/300 g fresh ginger,
   unpeeled
1 tablespoon gia vi (or a mix
   of 2 parts sugar, 1 part sea salt,
   1 part ground black pepper,
   1 part garlic powder)
1 tablespoon fish sauce
1 teaspoon granulated sugar
1 (8-ounce/220-g) can bamboo
   shoots, drained

Anh's mother is a real street-food veteran, and this recipe takes inspiration from a dish she used to make at her *bun cha* stall. The sweetness from the duck soaks into the bitterness of the bamboo shoots, but when you tuck into the noodle soup, everything is enveloped in a wholly different, very earthy flavor.

Rinse the duck under cold water. Rub it with salt, inside and out, and set it aside to rest at room temperature for 10 minutes. Then rinse it again in cold water and pat it dry with paper towels.

You can cook the duck whole or chop it into quarters. In a small bowl, combine the gia vi, pepper, ginger, and garlic, and rub the seasoning into the duck's skin.

In a large pan or lidded stockpot that is big enough to hold the duck, bring the hot water to a boil over high heat. Gently add the duck and bring the water back to a boil; reduce the heat to low, and cover the pan loosely with the lid, so there is enough steam for the duck to cook and enough escaping air to result in a clear broth. Cook for 45 to 60 minutes, until the meat is tender but not falling apart. When you insert a knife into the thickest part of the duck, the juices should run clear, and the internal temperature will be 185°F/85°C. Skim off any scum that appears on the surface of the liquid.

Remove the duck from the pot and soak it in a bowl of cold water for 5 minutes; remove it from the cold water and pat it dry with a paper towel.

Strain the duck broth into a clean stockpot.

To season the broth: If you have a gas stove, turn one of your burners to high flame. If you have an electric stove, preheat the broiler to high. Char the onion and ginger over the open flame or under the broiler for about 15 minutes, using tongs to rotate them occasionally until their skins burn and they become soft and fragrant. Alternatively, you can grill them for 15 minutes, turning them halfway through. Remove the charred skins, wash the onion and ginger, and add them whole to the broth.

**To assemble and serve
the bowls:**

1-2 packs rice vermicelli noodles

8 spring onions, chopped

1 red onion, sliced

1 bunch rau ram or mint, chopped

1 bunch cilantro, chopped

3 tablespoons Ginger and Dill
  Dipping Sauce (page 218)

Bring the broth to a simmer over medium-high heat and cook the broth for 15 minutes, then discard the onion and ginger. Season with the gia vi, fish sauce, and sugar. Add the bamboo shoots to the broth and bring it back to a boil.

To assemble the bowls: Cook the noodles according to the packet instructions, and then divide them evenly between your bowls.

Add a layer of duck to each bowl: you can shred the meat or just chop the duck into 6 pieces and serve it with the bone in. Add a layer of spring onion, sliced onion, and herbs. Ladle the bubbling broth into each bowl. Serve with the Ginger and Dill Dipping Sauce.

Note: You can also use a whole chicken for this recipe.

Social Cooking

(An Choi)

We grew up in Vietnam in the eighties, when doors were always wide open and we were as close to our neighbors as we were to our own relatives. The most joyous demonstration of this social living was the Lunar New Year of Tet, when the whole block would get together to cook an enormous Tet specialty cake on New Year's Eve. Over the three days of celebration, we would go from house to house, and each house would share a special dish they had cooked: things like sunflower seeds or candied winter melon, which were luxuries in those days. To many, the eighties might have seemed a bitter period for Vietnam. But for us two, it was the sweetest era, full of warmth and simplicity. Some might call us old romantics, to which I'd reply: it's a matter of perspective.

■ ■ ■ ■

Grapefruit and Shrimp Salad

SERVES 4

2 pomelos (or substitute red
  grapefruits)
12 jumbo shrimp, peeled, deveined,
  and steamed
8 tablespoons Garlic, Lime, and
  Chile Dipping Sauce (page 218)
2 tablespoons chopped fresh
  rau ram or cilantro

To garnish:
2 tablespoons roasted, salted
  peanuts, crushed
2 tablespoons dried shallots
  (or toasted dried onions)

This is a twist on a traditional Vietnamese recipe, which uses pomelo. Anh's mother would buy a farmer's basket full of pomelos at their ripest and store them in a nice cool place—under her bed to be precise—where they'd last through the winter. Pomelo has a gentler bitterness than grapefruit, but the latter's juiciness makes for a great local substitute. Or you might want to try this with a pomelo from a Turkish, Polish, or Asian grocer.

Peel the pomelos and be careful to remove all the white pith. Then separate the segments and take each segment out of its membrane: this is called supreming. Try to preserve them in chunks if you can.

Put the pomelos and shrimp in a large bowl and stir in the Garlic, Lime, and Chile dipping sauce. Stir in the chopped rau ram or cilantro. Spoon the salad onto individual plates and sprinkle peanuts and dried shallots over top.

Serve the salad on its own or with rice crackers.

Note: This recipe lends itself to adaptation. You can use other seafood, such as scallops or squid, and different fresh herbs, such as mint.

Deep-Fried Calamari with Ale

SERVES 4

For the batter:
2 cups/250 g tempura flour
    (or all-purpose flour)
1 egg yolk
2 cups/500 ml beer
3 tablespoons chopped fresh dill
2 tablespoons chopped
    fresh ginger

For the calamari:
14 ounces/400 g frozen squid rings,
    defrosted
½ tablespoon granulated sugar
½ teaspoon freshly ground
    black pepper
¼ tablespoon salt
Vegetable oil for frying

To serve:
Garlic, Lime, and Chile Dipping
    Sauce (page 218)
2 lemons, cut into wedges

When we go through a particularly unlucky spell, like the month when our delivery scooter got stolen in Brick Lane . . . and one of the kitchen staff badly cut his finger . . . and the stall's canopy at Berwick Street Market flew off and hit the environmental health officer . . . we Vietnamese eat a meal to erase the "bad luck." This meal typically involves squid, and here the mild bitterness of beer also helps drown our sorrows.

To make the batter: Put the tempura flour in a bowl, then pour in the egg yolk and mix well. Slowly add the beer, a little at a time, mixing constantly until the batter has the consistency of sauce; you may need to add a little water as well. Now mix in the dill and ginger.

To prepare the calamari: Rinse the squid in cold water; then drain the water and pat the squid dry with a paper towel. Put the squid in a bowl; add the sugar, pepper, and salt and shake well to mix.

Fill a heavy-bottomed pan or wok about a third full with oil and place it over medium-high heat. You'll know that the oil is hot enough when a little of the batter sizzles on first contact.

Dip the squid rings into the batter; let the excess batter drip off, and then fry the squid in batches for about a minute, until crisp and golden. As they are cooked, remove the calamari to a plate lined with a paper towel to drain.

Serve with the Garlic, Lime, and Chile Dipping Sauce and some lemon wedges for squeezing over the calamari.

Vietnamese Coffee with Condensed Milk

SERVES 1

Coffee beans
4 teaspoons hot water, plus more
    for brewing the coffee
4 teaspoons condensed milk
Ice cubes (optional)

When we opened our market cafe, No.101, in Shoreditch, we inherited an espresso machine, and, overnight, we were not just assembling baguettes but also churning out lattes. The shop had a large front window with a long counter, which became our favorite spot for watching the world go by. We could hardly tell if we were on the streets of Saigon or Shoreditch.

True Vietnamese coffee uses a slow-drip filter, called a phin filter, but you can use a stove-top espresso-maker for the closest similar result. The bitter coffee slowly seeps through the steel filter onto a thick layer of creamy condensed milk. To finish, we pour it into another glass with ice cubes, and the black and white merge into the distinctive *ca phe* color of Vietnamese iced coffee.

To prepare the black coffee: grind the coffee fresh, and pack it very tightly into a stovetop espresso maker. You'll need a couple of tablespoons total of ground coffee, approximately 1 ounce/20 g of coffee per serving. Fill the water compartment according to the manufacturer's directions, and set it over high heat.

Pour the 4 teaspoons of hot water into a small bowl, and pour in the condensed milk. The hot water will "cook" the condensed milk, but if you like your coffee black, skip the milk.

Once the coffee has bubbled into the top of the espresso maker, pour 2 to 3 ounces (65 to 90 ml) of espresso into the condensed milk mixture, depending on how strong you like your coffee. Drink the coffee hot, or if you prefer iced coffee, pour it over ice cubes and enjoy each sip.

Note: If you have a phin filter; set it over your coffee mug and fill it with ground coffee. Put the top of the phin in and press down lightly. Pour in 1 ounce/20 ml of boiling water and wait for it to be absorbed. Pour in another 2 ounces/45 ml of water and then put the lid on and wait. It's said that a good drip speed is one per second—it should take around 6 minutes.

Vietnamese Yogurt

1 (14-ounce/397-g) can
  condensed milk
1 full can boiling water
2 full cans milk
¾ can yogurt with active cultures

Vietnamese yogurt is smooth, silky, and set, with the distinct taste of condensed milk. It's easy to make and a world away from commercial brands. Once you've emptied the can of condensed milk, use the same can to measure out the water, milk, and yogurt starter.

Pour the condensed milk into a large bowl. Then fill up the same can with boiling water; swilling it around to dissolve the remaining milk. Pour the water into the bowl and stir so that the milk dissolves completely.

Measure out 2 cans of milk, pour them into the bowl, and stir again.

Measure out the yogurt, pour it into the bowl, and stir again. Do your best to stir until no or very few lumps remain.

Use a coarse mesh strainer lined with cheesecloth to strain the mixture twice.

Heat a kettle of water to about 160 to 175°F/70 to 80°C. If you don't have a thermometer, heat the water until there are small bubbles at the bottom of the pan, but don't allow it to boil. Turn off the heat. Set a deep, flat-lidded casserole or other lidded heatproof dish on the counter. It should be large enough to hold 6 to 8 single-serving ramekins without any tipping.

Divide the yogurt mixture among the 6 to 8 ramekins or heatproof jars. Place these in the casserole, and carefully pour the hot water into the casserole so that the water comes two-thirds of the way up the sides of the ramekins. Put a lid on the casserole, and then cover the whole thing with a towel or blanket for 8 to 10 hours. If it's very cold in your kitchen, change the hot water after 3 to 4 hours. The finished yogurt should settle and be very silky, smooth, and firm. You can keep one of your pots of yogurt for the next time so you don't ever have to buy yogurt again.

To serve, pour a shot of strong espresso, brewed Vietnamese-style if possible (page 162), over top of the yogurt.

Note: You can also use a yogurt machine, if you have one, following the manufacturer's instructions.

SALTINESS

&

HEALING

Chapter 5

Vietnamese are relatively simple people: sometimes it seems we lack the colorfulness of our neighbors. Vietnamese cooking is the same: we rely less on complex sauces and pastes, and more on the raw ingredients to bring out flavors. In fact, Vietnamese cooking principally uses only one sauce for marinating, cooking, seasoning and eating—and that's fish sauce. Everything else is a derivative of this liquid gold.

Anh and I got acquainted with the process of making fish sauce on our first trip to Phu Quoc island many moons ago. Phu Quoc is an island off the western coast of Vietnam in the bay of Thailand, renowned for the rich coral around the island, which the anchovies feed off, that makes the sauce so good. Good fish sauce should be made from only two ingredients—anchovies and salt—through a natural fermentation process. There are dozens of species of anchovies there, but only the islanders can tell the difference. The sauce is made in giant wooden vats, and the higher the protein level, the better the sauce. Through fermentation, the extracted fish sauce contain that elusive sixth flavor, umami, giving food a long-lasting, mouth-watering deliciousness that go beyond traditional flavor combinations.

The best fish sauce—virgin-pressed like olive oil—has up to 40 nitrogen grams per liter (40N). It should have a dark yet clear amber color and not contain additives such as MSG, soy, or flour. Good fish sauce has so much flavor that you can pour a spoonful over rice and just eat it like that, in the same way you might dip bread in olive oil. We use fish sauce as a substitute for salt, and go through a whole bottle every month. Pick up a bottle from an Asian supermarket or online and start experimenting: it will serve you well.

Some people think fish sauce stinks: we can't blame them when even Vietnam Airlines won't allow fish sauce on any of its flights. When we are in Phu Quoc in the villages where fish sauce factories are located, the air has a distinctive smell of fish sauce and sea salt. It's as if the whole village is enveloped in a fish sauce fume eternally. But we love fish sauce: it's our desert island cooking ingredient. It takes salt's temporary sprinkling impact and cultivates it into a more well-rounded flavor with a beautiful aftertaste. It cures anchovies into a concentrated flavor bomb that ages well regardless of the vintage. Like all good healers, fish sauce restores, nurtures, and brings everything back in balance.

Everyday Cooking
(An Com)

Vietnam has a very long sea coast, and harvesting sea salt is a tradition that has been around for thousands of years. Yet being blessed with this bounty from the sea doesn't mean salt is easy to harvest. In the old days, salt-makers often lost their feet from standing in the saline water for too long. And, even today, during the monsoon season, rain can suddenly descend on a field of harvested salt, melting it into water again, and wiping out a day's work in a blink.

Salt is, of course, part of everyday cooking. In Vietnam there are no fewer than 20 types: "live" salt fresh from the salt field; roasted salt; powdered salt; stewed salt; salt and pepper; salt and chile; salt and lemongrass; salt and galangal; salt and shrimp; salt and peanuts; salt and sesame; salt and garlic; and so on. In Hue there's a traditional meal called com muoi, which literally means rice and salt. It sounds so simple, it could be taken for peasant fare. But it's actually an elaborate feast reserved for special occasions—where the rice is served with more than ten kinds of flavored salt—to be shared only with close friends or lovers.

■ ■ ■ ■

Chargrilled Salmon with Ginger, Black Pepper, and Fish Sauce

SERVES 4

For the marinade:

1 (2-inch/6-cm) piece fresh ginger, peeled and thinly sliced

2 tablespoons fish sauce

1 teaspoon granulated sugar

2 teaspoons fresh lemon juice

2 teaspoons freshly ground black pepper

2 teaspoons crushed garlic

14 ounces/400 g skin-on salmon fillet, cut into 4 pieces

To garnish:

2 tablespoons chopped spring onion

2 tablespoons chopped fresh dill

On our first trip to the island of Phu Quoc, we headed south and stopped by a food stall on the beach. The stall belonged to a young woman, whose dog was running around on the beach while her son slept peacefully in a hammock. She served us the most delectable grilled fish, marinated in the island's own fish sauce. The fish tasted so fresh: it had come straight from the sea. Here, we've recreated the dish from memory, and added a kick of ginger and black pepper to balance the salty marinade.

In a large bowl, combine the ginger, fish sauce, sugar, lemon juice, pepper, and garlic. Add the salmon to the bowl and use a pastry brush to spread the marinade evenly over the salmon. Cover the bowl and place it in the fridge for 30 minutes.

If you are outdoors, cook the salmon on a charcoal grill (or gas barbecue) over medium heat for about 7 minutes on each side. Alternatively, preheat the oven to 400°F/200°C/gas 6 and bake the salmon on a foil-lined baking sheet for 8 to 12 minutes, or until done to your liking.

Scatter the spring onion and chopped dill over the salmon before serving.

Shoulder of Lamb with Vietnamese Miso

SERVES 6

18 ounces/1 kg boneless lamb shoulder

2 tablespoons vodka

1 tablespoon finely chopped fresh ginger

For the marinade:

5 tablespoons soybean paste

1 tablespoon finely chopped galangal (or fresh ginger)

1 tablespoon crushed garlic

½ tablespoon five spice powder

1 tablespoon fresh pear juice (substitute apple juice)

1 tablespoon finely chopped shallot

3 tablespoons sesame oil

1 tablespoon ground black pepper

½ tablespoon chili powder or ground paprika

Soybean paste, made from fermented soybeans, is widely used across Asia. The Japanese have their *miso*, the Koreans have their *ssamjang*, and the Vietnamese have their *tuong ban*. This marinade has an intense flavor and is one of Anh's more experimental recipes. For best results, try to source an authentic Vietnamese soybean paste in an Asian supermarket or online.

Cut the lamb into strips about 1 inch/2 cm thick.

In a large bowl, mix the vodka with the ginger and rub the mixture into the lamb strips. Then rinse the meat under cold running water and pat it dry with paper towels. This cleans the lamb and helps to remove the lamb's odor.

Combine the soybean paste, galangal, garlic, five spice powder, pear juice, shallot, sesame oil, pepper, and paprika in a large bowl or dish. Add the lamb, then cover the dish and place it in the fridge for an hour, or ideally overnight.

When ready to cook, thread the lamb pieces onto skewers, spreading them evenly along each skewer. Preheat a broiler or grill on high heat.

Cook under a hot broiler on a rack or roasting pan for 10 minutes on each side, or until done. You can also barbecue over a medium-hot charcoal grill or gas barbecue.

Chargrilled Sea Bass

SERVES 4

1 garlic clove, chopped

1 bird's-eye chile, finely chopped

1 (2-inch/5-cm) piece fresh ginger,
   peeled and roughly chopped

3 sprigs fresh dill, chopped

1 tablespoon granulated sugar

4 tablespoons fresh lemon juice

4 tablespoons water

2 tablespoons fish sauce,
   or to taste

1 whole sea bass
   (about 18 ounces/500 g), cleaned

2 lemongrass sticks, lightly crushed

This is another take on char-grilled fish. Here, the dill takes the dish in a whole new direction. Serve with potatoes and a simple salad for a stunning main course. Or strip off flakes of fish to put inside summer rolls (page 184).

In a small bowl, combine the garlic, chile, ginger, dill, sugar, lemon juice, and water. Add the fish sauce and stir until combined.

Place the fish in a baking dish. Using the point of a sharp knife, make 3 slits through the skin of the fish on each side. Pour a few teaspoons of the marinade inside the fish and fold the lemongrass into the cavity, then rub the remainder of the marinade all over the skin. Cover and leave to marinate for 20 to 30 minutes at room temperature. Preheat a broiler or a charcoal or gas grill on medium heat.

Uncover the fish and cook it under the broiler for 10 minutes on each side, or until thoroughly cooked. Alternatively, barbecue the fish on the grill for 10 minutes per side.

Chargrilled Sea Bass, page 175

Asparagus and Sprouting Broccoli with Peanuts and Black Sesame Salt

SERVES 4

2 tablespoons salted roasted
   peanuts

1 tablespoon sea salt

1 tablespoon sesame seeds

1 teaspoon unsalted butter

2 tablespoons dried shallots
   (or toasted dried onion)

7 ounces/200 g asparagus tips

7 ounces/200 g purple sprouting
   broccoli

The sea salt, ground peanut, and sesame seed mix used here makes a simple but magical seasoning that can be used in a variety of dishes. In our schooldays, sometimes our packed lunches would simply be rice pressed into dumplings and then dipped in this peanut-sesame mix.

Crush the roasted peanuts with the sea salt in a mortar and pestle (or use a grinder or food processor) until they are coarsely ground. Add the sesame seeds and pound again, then mix well.

Set a frying pan over medium heat and add the butter. Add the dried shallots and toss for a couple of minutes until they are golden, crispy, and fragrant. Pour this shallot butter into a jug or bowl and set aside.

Add the asparagus and the sprouting broccoli to the same frying pan and stir-fry them for a couple of minutes until they are crisp-tender—they will cook faster if you put a lid on the pan.

Remove the asparagus and sprouting broccoli to a serving plate. Drizzle the shallot butter and sprinkle the peanut and sesame salt mixture over the vegetables, and serve.

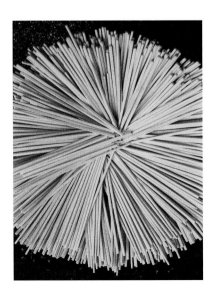

Festive Cooking

(An Qua)

In this section we've included a banh mi baguette recipe that we call Fish Q. The inspiration for this came from a cult dish that you could find in only one restaurant in the Old Quarter of Hanoi: fish cooked in hot oil at your table. We only ate there when my father had special visitors in town, and that dish was one of the true treats of my childhood. I described the taste to Anh and, before I knew it, Fish Q was on our menu even though she hadn't even tasted the original dish. This is typical of the way we operate: we imagine how a dish tastes when we might only have read about it, or seen a picture, or literally dreamt it. And then we experiment in the kitchen, tasting our way until we hit the right notes. There are parts of Vietnam we've never explored and dishes we've never tasted, so our cooking is not just about replication, but imagination.

Intuition and versatility are always useful in cooking, but for us they are indispensable, because we are taking an age-old ethnic cuisine and attempting to make it work in modern kitchens.

■ ■ ■ ■

Hanoi Shrimp Fritters
(Banh Tom)

This is our interpretation of a dish familiar to anyone from Hanoi: the shrimp fritter of West Lake. West Lake is like a village made up only of restaurants, and to visit there is embark on a food pilgrimage.

MAKES 12 FRITTERS

For the batter:
1 or 2 small sweet potatoes, about
    11 ounces/300 g total
2 egg yolks
1⅛ cups/200 g all-purpose flour
¾ cup/100 g rice flour
1 teaspoon granulated sugar
2 tablespoons water
½ teaspoon salt
½ teaspoon gia vi (or a mix
    of 2 parts sugar, 1 part sea salt,
    1 part ground black pepper,
    1 part garlic powder)

For the marinade:
1 teaspoon crushed garlic
1 teaspoon freshly ground
    black pepper
1 teaspoon gia vi (or a mix
    of 2 parts sugar, 1 part sea salt,
    1 part ground black pepper,
    1 part garlic powder)
1 tablespoon fish sauce
½ teaspoon sugar
18 ounces/500 g peeled fresh
    shrimp

To make the batter: Peel the sweet potatoes and shred them into long strips using a grater or food processor.

In a large bowl, mix the egg yolks with the flours and the sugar. Add the water, salt, and gia vi. Add the potato strips to the batter. Cover the bowl and place it in the fridge for 30 minutes.

To make the marinade: Combine the garlic, pepper, gia vi, fish sauce, and sugar in a bowl. Add the shrimp and let it marinate at room temperature for 20 minutes.

To make the dipping sauce: Shred the papaya (if using) and carrot into thin ribbons using a box grater or a food processor with the grating attachment. Fill a bowl with cold water and 1 teaspoon of salt, and soak the ribbons for 10 minutes. Drain the papaya and carrot and set them on paper towels to dry.

Put the shredded papaya and carrot into a large bowl. Add the remaining teaspoon of salt and squeeze the shredded papaya and carrot with your hands. Add the sugar and the rice vinegar and let the mixture sit for 15 minutes at room temperature. This will lightly pickle the vegetables.

Add the pickled vegetables to a large bowl along with the dipping sauce, and stir to combine.

For the dipping sauce:

¼ green papaya (optional)

1 carrot

2 teaspoons salt, divided

1 teaspoon granulated sugar

2 teaspoons rice vinegar

1 recipe Garlic, Lime, and Chile
Dipping Sauce (page 218)

To cook the fritters:

7 ounces/200 ml vegetable oil

1 garlic clove, sliced

To serve:

1 head butter lettuce, leaves torn

A few sprigs mint

A few sprigs cilantro

A few sprigs basil

To cook the fritters: Heat the oil in a frying pan over medium heat, throw in the sliced garlic, and stir quickly until the oil is fragrant, about 1 minute. Add the marinated shrimp and cook for a couple of minutes until they turn pink. Don't overcook the shrimp, since they will also be fried. Do not clean out the pan, and keep it over medium heat.

Roughly form a single 2-inch/5 cm-long layer of battered potato strips on a metal slotted spoon or spatula. Lower the spoon or spatula into the hot oil in the skillet for a couple of minutes until it turns golden brown. Lift the spoon out of the oil and lay a couple of shrimp on top of the fried potato, then submerge it in the oil again for a couple of minutes to finish cooking. Remove the fritter to a plate lined with paper towels. Next, fry another single layer of potato strips and sandwich this on top of the prawns. It should now look like a prawn toast, using sweet potato for the sandwich.

Repeat the process and you should have roughly 12 fritters in total.

Wrap each fritter in a lettuce leaf with a little mint, cilantro, and basil, and serve alongside the vegetable dipping sauce.

Note: Green papaya is a special variety found in Asian supermarkets. Don't use yellow papaya, as it will disintegrate.

Shrimp Summer Rolls

MAKES 10
SUMMER ROLLS

⅓ cup/100 ml coconut milk
1 lemongrass stick (optional)
10 cooked and peeled
   large shrimp

**For assembling the
summer rolls:**
10 sheets rice paper
3½ ounces/100 g rice vermicelli
   noodles, cooked according to
   packet instructions (about a
   quarter of a packet of noodles)
1 head butter lettuce
1 large carrot, peeled and shredded
1 cucumber, cut into matchsticks
½ pineapple, peeled, cored,
   and cut into matchsticks
1 bunch cilantro

To serve:
Garlic, Lime, and Chile Dipping
   Sauce (page 218)

Summer rolls are amazingly fresh and delicious. I'd like to think that in ten years, they will be as widely available as sushi is now. The basics you will need are rice paper wraps, fresh herbs, and a pinch of cooked vermicelli noodles. On top of that you can experiment with pretty much any fillings. The dipping sauces are equally imaginative, from peanut sauce to garlic and lime. It's a gorgeous way to pack so many fresh flavors in one bite. Rolling them can be tricky at first, but after a couple of goes you'll crack it. Children are good at making summer rolls! This recipe makes a fun family activity, rolling and eating at the table together.

In a large saucepan over medium-high heat, heat the coconut milk and bring to a simmer. Add the lemongrass stick (if using) and the shrimp, and cook for 2 to 3 minutes or until the shrimp is pink and cooked through. Discard the lemongrass, drain the shrimp, and set them aside to cool at room temperature.

To assemble the summer rolls: Set out a chopping board covered with a tea towel or muslin cloth. Fill a deep dish or wide bowl with warm water. Submerge the rice papers in the water for a couple of seconds, and lift them out. Place the rice papers on the towel-lined board in a single layer. Place a pinch of cooked noodles on the center of one sheet. Add a lettuce leaf, then a pinch of shredded carrot and a stick each of cucumber and pineapple. Roll the rice paper over once.

Cut the shrimp in half lengthwise and place one half neatly on the rice paper with a sprig of cilantro.

Fold the two sides of the rice paper in and roll up the whole length of the paper. Repeat until you are out of papers and fillings.

Serve the summer rolls with the dipping sauce.

Note: You can make summer rolls with any other meat or fish instead of shrimp. Using this recipe, you could also add chive and thin slices of boiled pork belly for a classic Saigon street-food version. Our favorite filling for a family feast is the Chargrilled Sea Bass from page 175.

Making Summer and Spring Rolls

After experimenting with several types of rice paper for summer rolls, we finally figured out that the simplest way to prepare the rice paper is to submerge it in warm water before rolling. This makes it very soft and easy to work with, and the water evaporates quickly so that the rice paper is not soaked.

Put less filling on the rice paper than you think you'll need, then roll almost to the end of the paper, fold in the sides, and roll over again.

We wrap our summer rolls in round lettuce leaves before eating them so they retain their moisture.

You can use this same technique with rice paper for spring rolls, but layer the rice paper between lettuce leaves the night before you want to roll them: this will introduce moisture gradually to soften them. In Vietnam we use banana leaves, but any type of leafy vegetable should do the trick. This gives the rice paper just enough moisture to make it easier to work with, but not so much that it disintegrates as you roll.

Pork Spring Rolls
(Pork Nem)

MAKES 20 ROLLS

For the filling:
2 carrots
2 ounces/50 g dried shiitake
    mushrooms
2 ounces/50g dried wood ear
    mushrooms (or use another
    2 ounces/50g shiitake)
3½ ounces/100g glass noodles
11 ounces/300 g ground pork
1 teaspoon freshly ground black
    pepper
1 tablespoon fish sauce
11 ounces/100 g fresh white
    crabmeat
1 teaspoon finely chopped shallot
1 teaspoon finely chopped garlic
3 to 4 teaspoons chopped
    spring onion
2 eggs

For assembling and frying:
1 tablespoon vinegar
6 tablespoons/100 ml water
20 sheets rice paper
Vegetable oil for frying

To serve:
Garlic, Lime, and Chile Dipping
    Sauce (page 218)

Nem, as we call a spring roll in the north of Vietnam, is a food that is served at family feasts like weddings and anniversaries. Eating nem is one of our earliest childhood memories, and it reminds us of the excitement of large family get-togethers. This recipe is how our mothers taught us to make it, although we never seem to get the rolls as perfectly crispy as they did!

To make the filling: Peel the carrots, and shred them into long slithers, using a box grater or a food processor with the grating attachment.

In a medium bowl, soak the shiitake and wood ear mushrooms in hot water for about 15 minutes. Drain and pat them dry with a paper towel, then slice them thinly.

In another medium bowl, soak the glass noodles in cold water for about 15 minutes, then drain them and cut them into 2-inch/5-cm lengths.

In a large bowl, mix the pork with the pepper and fish sauce. Stir in the crabmeat, working it well into the mixture with a wooden spoon or rubber spatula. Add the mushrooms and noodles. Add the carrot together with the shallot, garlic, and spring onion. Crack the eggs into the mixture, and stir well. Set the bowl aside until you are ready to assemble the rolls.

When you are ready to roll, mix together the vinegar and water in a small bowl. Set out a chopping board covered with a tea towel or muslin cloth. Fill a deep dish or wide bowl with lukewarm water. Submerge the rice papers in the lukewarm water for a couple of seconds, and lift out. Place the rice papers on the towel-lined board in a single layer.

Our mothers' trick is to first fold over the rice paper once, then put about 2 tablespoons of filling on the folded part. Now roll twice almost to the end of the rice paper; then fold the two sides in and roll again. Your finished rolls will be about 4 inches (10 cm) long. Brush on some of the vinegar and water to seal the fold. Repeat with the remaining papers and filling.

(Recipe continues)

To fry the spring rolls: Heat 1 inch of oil in a small, heavy-bottomed pan or deep frying pan. When the oil is hot, gently add the rolls, one at a time, turning them once in the oil to coat. Cook the rolls evenly on all sides, about 8 minutes total for each roll. The rolls should be golden-brown on all sides but not burned or blistered. Carefully remove the cooked rolls to a plate lined with paper towels to drain.

The dipping sauce is best served warm: To do this, pour it into a heat-safe bowl and microwave it slightly before serving. Serve the spring rolls with the dipping sauce.

Fish Spring Rolls
(*Fish Nem*)

MAKES 15 TO 20 ROLLS

For the filling:

11 ounces/300 g skinless sea
    bass fillet

1 teaspoon crushed garlic

2 teaspoons grated fresh ginger

2 tablespoons chopped fresh dill

1 teaspoon freshly ground
    black pepper

1 tablespoon fish sauce

1 carrot, peeled

For assembling and frying:

1 tablespoon vinegar

6 tablespoons/100 ml water

15 to 20 sheets rice paper

Vegetable oil for frying

To serve:

Ginger and Dill Dipping Sauce
    (page 218)

We came up with this dish for our pop-up supper clubs. To accommodate an array of food allergies and dietary requirements, we made almost all the menu seafood. Nem is traditionally made with ground pork, but we like using sea bass, too, for its texture, although you could substitute with any other firm fish. This recipe nods to the past while experimenting in the present.

To make the filling: Use a food processor to mince the sea bass fillet until it forms an elastic paste. Transfer the paste to a large bowl, and mix in the garlic, ginger, dill, black pepper, and fish sauce. Grate the carrot and add it to the mix Set the filling aside until you are ready to assemble the rolls (see note).

When you are ready to roll, mix together the vinegar and water in a small bowl. Set out a chopping board covered with a tea towel or muslin cloth. Fill a deep dish or wide bowl with lukewarm water. Submerge the rice paper in the lukewarm water for a couple of seconds, and lift out. Place the rice papers on the towel-lined board in a single layer. Work with one sheet of rice paper at a time. First fold over the rice paper once, then put a generous tablespoon of the filling on the folded part. Now roll twice almost to the end of the rice paper, and then fold the two sides in and roll again. Using a pastry brush, brush on some of the vinegar-water to seal the fold. Repeat with the remaining sheets and filling.

To fry the spring rolls: Heat 1 inch of oil in a small, heavy-bottomed pan or deep frying pan. When the oil is hot, gently add the rolls, one at a time, turning them once in the oil to coat. Cook the rolls evenly on all sides, about 8 minutes total for each roll. The rolls should be golden-brown on all sides but not burned or blistered. Carefully remove the cooked rolls to a plate lined with paper towels to drain.

(Recipe continues)

The dipping sauce is best served warm: to do this, pour it into a heat-safe bowl and microwave it slightly before serving. Serve the spring rolls with the dipping sauce.

Note: The key to making spring rolls crispy is to ensure that all the ingredients are dry. It's therefore a good idea to prepare the filling in advance and let it air-dry in a colander for about 20 minutes before rolling and frying the spring rolls just before serving.

Shrimp Summer Rolls in Sweetheart Cabbage

SERVES 4

1 sweetheart (pointed) cabbage, about 2¼ to 2¾ inches/6 to 7 cm in length

7 ounces/200 g lean pork belly

Pinch of salt

1 scant inch/2 cm fresh ginger, peeled and sliced

6 tablespoons/100 ml coconut milk

1 stalk lemongrass, chopped (20 g)

7 ounces/200 g peeled fresh shrimp

1 egg

1 tablespoon vegetable oil

5 ounces/150 g Vietnamese pork ham (optional)

1 to 2 bunches chives or spring onions

½ (14-ounce/400-g) pack rice vermicelli noodles

Peanut Dipping Sauce (page 220)

The traditional recipe uses mustard greens for a tangy and fresh taste. However, as these are not readily available in some supermarkets year-round, we've substituted it with sweetheart cabbage. Chinese cabbage would also work well.

Cut the cabbage in half, remove and discard the hard core, and separate the leaves. Fill a large bowl with ice water and set it aside. Bring a large pot of water to a boil, add the cabbage leaves, and cook for about 5 minutes, then, using tongs, transfer the leaves to the ice water to soak for about 2 minutes. Do not drain the hot water from the pot. Drain the leaves and set them aside to dry on paper towels.

Bring the water back to a boil in the same large pot, add the pork belly with a pinch of salt and the slices of ginger, and reduce to a simmer. Cook for about 30 minutes. The meat should remain submerged in the water for the entire cooking time; add more water as needed. Remove the pork to a chopping board; cool slightly, pat dry, and then cut the pork into slices about ½ inch/1 cm in width.

Wash out the pot and return it to the stove. Pour in the coconut milk, add the lemongrass, and bring the mixture to a boil. Add the shrimp and cook until they turn pink. Immediately drain the shrimp in a colander, then rinse them quickly under cold water and set them aside to dry on paper towels.

In a small bowl, whisk the egg. Heat the oil in a frying pan over medium-high heat, then quickly pour in the egg and swirl it around the pan to coat evenly, to make a very thin omelet (like a pancake). Remove the cooked egg to a plate, and slice it into long, thin strips.

Prepare the pork ham (if using) by slicing it into long, thin strips.

(Recipe continues)

Bring a small pot of water to a boil over high heat. Cut the chives or spring onions into 4-inch/10-cm lengths and blanch them in the boiling water for 2 to 3 minutes.

Cook the rice noodles according to the packet instructions, then drain and set them aside to dry.

To assemble the rolls, lay a cabbage leaf flat on a chopping board and put a teaspoonful of rice noodles on it. Top with 1 to 2 shrimp and a couple of slices of egg, pork ham, and pork belly. Then roll up the cabbage leaf and tie it with a length of chive or spring onion. Use scissors to trim the ends of the roll. Repeat with the remaining cabbage leaves and filling.

Serve the rolls with the Peanut Dipping Sauce.

Fish Q Vietnamese Baguette
(*Banh Mi*)

SERVES 4

For the fish:

14 ounces/400 g firm skinless
   whitefish fillet (sea bass, whiting,
   cod, or catfish), deboned
⅔ cup/160 ml vegetable oil, divided
2 tablespoons finely chopped
   shallots
2 tablespoons crushed garlic
2 tablespoons finely chopped fresh
   galangal (or ginger)
1 tablespoon shrimp paste
2 tablespoons fresh lemon juice
2 tablespoons granulated sugar
1 tablespoon gia vi (or a mix
   of 2 parts sugar, 1 part sea salt,
   1 part ground black pepper,
   1 part garlic powder)
2 tablespoons fish sauce
2 tablespoons ground turmeric
1 tablespoon plain yogurt
2 bunches fresh dill, chopped
1 spring onion, chopped

We tested endless recipes for a fish banh mi, before I finally thought of the dish from the restaurant my father took me to as a childhood treat: fish cooked at the table in hot oil. The pungent marinade on that fish was an acquired taste. It was also out of the reach of my father's pockets most of the time, as it was one of the most expensive meals in Hanoi's Old Quarter at that time. But I never forgot it.

For the recipe here, we finally cracked the marinade, and then we introduced red onion and peanuts for a banh mi–style crunch to complement the delicate fish.

To prepare the fish: Cut the fish fillets into 1-inch/2.5-cm cubes.

Put 4 tablespoons of the oil in a frying pan over medium heat. When the oil is hot, add the shallots, garlic, and galangal. Toss until fragrant for 1 minute, then remove the pan from the heat and transfer the vegetables to a large bowl.

In a separate small bowl, add the shrimp paste and slowly stir in the lemon juice, mixing well in a circular motion. You should see some small white bubbles as you mix them together. Stir in the sugar and let the mixture rest for a moment.

Take the bowl of shallots, garlic, and ginger; mix in the gia vi and fish sauce, then add the shrimp paste mixture and mix well. Finally, add the turmeric and yogurt and stir again until well combined.

Add the fish cubes to this marinade and massage the fish so that it absorbs the marinade. Cover the bowl with plastic wrap and put it in the fridge for a couple of hours.

When you are ready to cook the fish, preheat a charcoal or gas grill on medium-high heat (or preheat a broiler on high). Grill or broil the marinated fish for 5 to 10 minutes on each side, or until thoroughly cooked (depending on your broiler, it may take more or less time).

For assembling the banh mi:

2 baguettes, each about
  8 inches/20 cm long
1 tablespoon mayonnaise
Carrot and Daikon Pickles
  (page 215)
Red Onion Pickles, to taste
  (page 214)
10 cucumber slices
4 fresh sprigs cilantro

To garnish:

2 tablespoons roasted, salted
  crushed peanuts
Chopped fresh chiles or chili sauce,
  to taste

Heat the remaining 6 tablespoons of oil in a frying pan over medium-high heat. When the oil is hot, add the dill and spring onion and toss until they are softened but still green. Now add the cooked fish in batches and toss again to briefly crisp in the oil. You can add extra oil if needed.

To assemble the banh mi: Slice the baguettes lengthways on the diagonal. Spread the mayo evenly on both sides of each roll. Spread Carrot and Daikon Pickles and Red Onion Pickles to taste along the bread. Add the fish with the dill and spring onion. Add the cucumber and cilantro sprigs. Sprinkle some crushed peanuts over, to finish. If you wish, you can add chopped fresh chiles or chile sauce, to taste.

Social Cooking
(An Choi)

A salty flavor lends itself perfectly to small plates, like the salads and snacks included here. Simple to execute and effective: what's not to like about a sea bass carpaccio or a chicory and tofu salad?

■ ■ ■ ■

Chicory and Tofu Salad with Sesame, Soy, and Ginger Dressing

SERVES 2

For the salad:
7 ounces/200 g soft tofu
1 head chicory
1 pomegranate
1 bunch watercress

For the dressing:
2 tablespoons granulated sugar
4 tablespoons warm water
4 tablespoons soy sauce
1 teaspoon grated fresh ginger
1 tablespoon sesame oil
Juice of 1 clementine

This is one of the most fabulous salads we have "cooked," although cooking is an overstatement because it's beyond simple to put together.

Cut the tofu into small cubes, about the same size as sugar cubes. Separate the chicory leaves and wash them. Cut the pomegranate in half and remove the seeds.

For the dressing, put the sugar and water in a heavy-bottomed pan over a medium heat until the sugar has completely dissolved. Stir in the soy sauce, ginger, and sesame oil. Cut the clementine in half and squeeze the juice into the pan.

To assemble the salad: Arrange the chicory leaves in a flower petal configuration on individual serving plates. Spoon the tofu cubes over the leaves, sprinkle the watercress on top. Drizzle the dressing over the salad and top with the pomegranate seeds.

Sea Bass Carpaccio

SERVES 4

For the fish:
1 sea bass fillet (about 11
   ounces/300 g), skinned
2 tablespoons fresh lime juice

For the shallot oil:
2 tablespoons vegetable oil
1 tablespoon dried shallots
   (or toasted dried onions)

To serve:
1 recipe Ginger and Dill Dipping
   Sauce (page 218)
A few cilantro leaves,
   to garnish

I've always thought Italian and Vietnamese food have much in common. Both countries are long and boot-shaped, with diverse regional cuisines and a big appetite for food. This is one of the most obvious examples of how the two styles cross over.

To prepare the fish: Cut the sea bass fillet in half lengthways and then cut each half widthwise into thin (⅛-inch/3-mm-thick) slices. This is easy to do if you partially freeze it first (see page 231).

Place the sea bass slices on a plate in a single layer and drizzle the lime juice over them. Set aside.

To make the shallot oil: Put the vegetable oil in a frying pan set over a medium heat. When the oil is hot, add the dried shallots and sauté for about 1 to 2 minutes until they are golden and crispy. Carefully pour the shallots with their oil into a heatproof bowl and set aside.

To serve: Pour the dipping sauce into a shallow bowl. Add the sea bass slices to the dipping sauce; leave them in the sauce for about 1 minute, then remove them to a serving plate, arranging the slices in a single layer. Drizzle some shallot oil over the carpaccio and garnish with cilantro leaves.

Fresh Shrimp Steamed in Beer with Chile-Lime Dipping Sauce

This is a quick recipe that's perfect with a glass of cold beer.

SERVES 4

For the shrimp:

1 (12-ounce/330-ml) bottle of light or lager beer

1 bunch fresh lemongrass

2¼ pounds/1 kg fresh shrimp, shells on

Pinch of sea salt

For the dipping sauce:

3 tablespoons coarse sea salt

2 tablespoons freshly ground black pepper

Juice of 1 lime

3 teaspoons finely chopped bird's eye chiles, or to taste

To prepare the shrimp: Reserve a tablespoon of the beer in a small bowl, then pour the rest of the beer into the bottom of a large stockpot or Dutch oven. Place the pot over medium-high heat and bring the beer to a boil.

Using a rolling pin or the broad side of a knife, crush the lemongrass stalks. Lay the crushed lemongrass in a steamer basket or metal colander and sit it above the boiling beer in the pot. Arrange the shrimp on top of the lemongrass.

Sprinkle a pinch of sea salt and the reserved tablespoon of beer over the shrimp, then cover the pot and steam the shrimp for around 5 to 7 minutes, or until the shrimp turn pink.

Tip the shrimp into a serving bowl and discard the lemongrass and beer.

To make the dipping sauce: Mix the sea salt and ground pepper in a medium bowl. Squeeze the lime juice into the bowl and mix well. Finally, add chopped chile to taste. Now you are ready to start peeling, dipping, and eating your shrimp!

Baked Sweet Potato with Peanut Crème Fraîche

SERVES 1

1 sweet potato
2 tablespoons crème fraîche
1 tablespoon ground
  salted peanuts

Sweet potato and corn on the cob are the favorite late-night snacks in Vietnam. Around ten o'clock in the evening, street vendors peddle their bicycles around the neighborhoods and shout out their wares. There the sweet potato is nibbled on its own, but here we've souped it up with crème fraîche and salty peanuts. You could also chargrill the sweet potato instead of baking it, perfect for a summer evening in the back garden.

Preheat the oven to 400°F/200°C/gas 6.

Cut the sweet potato in half, wrap each half in foil, and bake it in the oven for about 45 minutes or until soft.

Mix the crème fraîche with the peanuts and spoon the mixture over the potato halves. Serve right away.

Sweet Corn with Sesame Butter

SERVES 1

1 ear sweet corn, husked
1 tablespoon unsalted butter,
   at room temperature
Sesame seeds, as needed

This light snack is also inspired by the cobs served by peddlers bicycling through the empty streets of late-night Vietnam. We've brightened it here with a spoonful of butter and a sprinkling of sesame seeds. Pick up a couple of cobs from the market in the summer, when they are freshly harvested and full of flavor.

Preheat the oven to 375°F/180°C/gas 4.

Put the corn in a small baking dish. Use a brush to spread the butter all over the corn. Bake the corn in the oven for 15 minutes, turning it once halfway through. When the corn is crisp-tender, sprinkle the sesame seeds on top and serve.

VIETNAMESE
PANTRY
ESSENTIALS

MASTER RECIPES

Annatto Seed Oil

Annatto seed oil adds color and fragrance to a dish, while remaining neutral in taste.

MAKES ⅓ CUP/100 ML

⅓ cup/100 ml vegetable oil
½ teaspoon annatto seeds

Heat the oil in a frying pan over medium-high heat until it is hot but not smoking. To test the heat of the oil, throw one annatto seed into the pot; if it sizzles and bubbles immediately on contact with the oil, the oil is hot enough. Now you can add the remaining annatto seeds to the oil. Cook for 2 to 3 minutes until fragrant, stirring constantly so the seeds don't burn.

Turn off the heat and let the oil cool a little at room temperature. Then carefully strain the oil through a fine-mesh sieve into a jar or other airtight container, and discard the seeds. You will have an orange-colored oil with fragrance from the annatto seeds.

This will keep in a jar at room temperature for up to 2 months.

Broth

Broth is a cornerstone of Vietnamese cooking because it is the basis of noodle soups. Homemade broth takes a long time to make, but it is worth it! Once you have created a flavorful broth you have laid the foundation for an amazing meal. Whatever you then do with that broth is really just a form of garnishing. Broth is the Vietnamese equivalent of European stock, and, as with stock, you can strain and freeze broth. We often just leave the bones in the bottom of the stockpot, though, and make sure not to ladle them when we pour out bowls of noodle soup. If you want to make broth in bulk just double all of the listed ingredients.

Beef Broth

**MAKES ABOUT
8 CUPS/2 L**

4 quarts/4 L water, divided
2 tablespoons salt, divided
1 cup/230 g sliced fresh ginger,
     divided
4¼ pounds/2 kg beef bones

In a large stockpot over high heat, bring 8 cups/2 L of water to a boil, and add ½ tablespoon of the salt and ¼ cup/50 g of the sliced ginger.

When the water comes to a boil, add the beef bones, reduce the heat to medium, and bring the water back to a boil. After about 5 minutes, drain the water and rinse the bones under cold water.

Use a small, sharp knife to remove any residual meat or muscles from the bones; use a small spoon to scoop out the bone marrow, and discard. Place the clean bones in a large bowl along with another ½ tablespoon of salt and another ¼ cup of sliced ginger, and fill the bowl with cold water.

In a large, clean stockpot over high heat, bring the remaining 8 cups/2 L of water to a boil and add the remaining ½ cup of sliced ginger and the remaining 1 tablespoon of salt.

Once the water is boiling, add the clean beef bones and reduce the heat until the water's at an almost imperceptible simmer. You should see tiny bubbles. Watch the pot carefully, as if the heat is too high, the stock will be cloudy.

Cook for as long as you can, at least 4 hours. As the broth reduces, top it up with more hot water to maintain the original water level.

Once done, you can transfer the broth to a large container and store it in the fridge for up to 5 days. You can also freeze it for later use.

Chicken Broth

MAKES ABOUT 2 QUARTS/2 L

1 chicken carcass or 11 ounces/300 g chicken bones
2 tablespoons salt, divided
2 quarts/2 L water
½ cup/100 grams sliced fresh ginger

To clean the chicken carcass, first rinse it under cold running water. Then rub 1 tablespoon of salt into the carcass and rinse it again.

In a large stockpot over high heat, bring the water to a boil and add the ginger and the remaining 1 tablespoon of salt. Once the water comes to a boil, put the chicken carcass in, ensuring that there's enough water to submerge the carcass and cover by a generous inch/3 cm.

Reduce the heat to low so that the water is at a bare simmer. Leave the pot uncovered, and cook for 2 hours. Top it off with more hot water as needed to maintain the original water level. Use a spoon to gently skim off any foam or fat that surfaces, keeping the stock clear. Strain the finished stock and refrigerate it in an airtight container for up to 3 days. You can also freeze it for later use.

Vegetable Broth

MAKES ABOUT 2 QUARTS/2 L

2 carrots
1 celery root
1 rutabaga
½ daikon radish (optional)
2 quarts/2 L water
1 teaspoon salt

Peel the vegetables, and then cut them into large chunks.

In a large stockpot, bring the water to a boil over high heat and add the salt. Once the water is boiling, add the vegetable chunks, ensuring that there's enough water to submerge the vegetables.

Bring the water back to a boil, then reduce the heat to medium-low and cook for 45 minutes to an hour. The longer you cook the vegetables, the sweeter the broth will taste. Strain the finished broth into an airtight container, discarding the vegetables, and refrigerate the broth for up to 3 days. You can also freeze it for later use.

Caramel Water

MAKES ABOUT
1 CUP/240 ML

¼ cup/50 g granulated sugar
1 cup/240 ml hot water

Caramel is a fundamental ingredient in clay pot cooking and grilling, and adds a concentrated, but not saccharine, sweetness to marinades. Melting the sugar removes water and intensifies its flavors. This caramel water has a more liquid consistency than the caramel sauce used for braising.

Place a heavy-bottomed pan over a medium heat. Make sure there's no water residue in the pan before you add the sugar—if necessary, wipe out the pan with a paper towel.

Pour the sugar into the pan and keep it over medium heat, without stirring, for 2 to 3 minutes, to melt the sugar. You can shake the pan slightly so the sugar spreads out and melts evenly.

Once the sugar starts to foam and the clumpy crystals melt, lower the heat and stir constantly with a wooden spoon, to ensure there is no burned sugar at the bottom. The sugar will become pale amber or golden brown in color: this is the color you want. Immediately pour in the hot water and stir again. The water will foam and the sugar will harden, but keep stirring and it will melt into a smooth liquid.

Cook until the caramel starts to boil, then remove the pan from the heat and let the syrup come to room temperature.

Pour the syrup into an airtight container and store it for up to one week in the fridge.

Note: Hot water helps the sugar to caramelize faster and results in a more pronounced flavor: There will inevitably be some foaming as the caramel boils, so be careful. It's best not to let the caramel get too dark and to err on the lighter brown side before pouring in the water; otherwise the sugar will burn very quickly and build up steam in minutes.

Pickle Brine

MAKES ABOUT 1 SCANT CUP/200 ML

2 tablespoons granulated sugar
1 tablespoon gia vi (or a mix
  of 2 parts sugar, 1 part sea salt,
  1 part ground black pepper,
  1 part garlic powder)
½ cup/100 ml lukewarm water
½ cup/100 ml lemon juice

When we started making carrot and daikon pickles for banh mi, we tried various techniques for making pickling brine and discovered that it doesn't have to be complicated. We stopped using vinegar, because it was hard to find natural rice vinegar from fermented rice, not chemicals, and the pickles in vinegar brine came out stark and sour. So we decided to use lemon juice. Lemons have a clear, crisp, and mild sourness and preserve vegetables beautifully. The sourness from vinegar is more acidic, and therefore can be very sharp, so if you prefer to substitute vinegar in this recipe you may want to add more sugar to the recipe to balance out the sourness.

In a sealed nonreactive container or large sterilized jar (page 134), dissolve the sugar and gia vi in the lukewarm water, stirring until there are no visible grains of sugar in the mixture. Add the lemon juice and mix well.

Use this as a brine for any sliced vegetable. Just add the vegetables to the container, making sure they are fully submerged in the brine. Screw on the lid or cover the container and let the pickles sit in the refrigerator for at least 12 hours or overnight before using.

Red Onion Pickles

**MAKES ABOUT 2
CUPS/500 G**

1 pound/450 g red onions
4 cups/1 L hot water
1 recipe Pickle Brine (page 213)

We use these pickles as an accompaniment to our Fish Q banh mi (page 196) on our market stall menu, and they always attract a lot of attention. They're also great with fish and grilled meat.

Cut the red onions into quarters, and then cut the quarters into thin slices. Place the onion slices in a large bowl. Pour the hot water over the onions, and let them sit for a few minutes at room temperature before draining them. This will soften and slightly cook the onions, so they will last longer and absorb the brine better. You don't want them too soft, though; they should still be crunchy when you drain them.

Drain the onions and transfer them to another large bowl. Add the pickle brine and mix well. Transfer the onions and brine to a sealed nonreactive container or sterilized jars (page 134), making sure that the onions are fully submerged in the brine. Leave the pickles in the fridge overnight before using.

To serve, squeeze out any residual brine. The pickles will keep for up to 2 weeks in the fridge.

Carrot and Daikon Pickles

MAKES ABOUT 3 CUPS/700 G

1 pound/450 g carrots
½ pound/200 g daikon radish (or substitute with more carrots)
4 cups/1 L hot water
1 teaspoon salt
1 recipe Pickle Brine (page 213)

Carrot and daikon is the classic pickle combination. The ingredients are easily available and they sit beautifully in a jam jar in the fridge for a few weeks. We add them as the staple pickle for banh mi and noodle salad recipes, but they are also perfect on their own to add more crunch as a side dish or to munch on as an appetizer.

Peel the carrots and daikon radish. Use a grater or vegetable peeler to shave off thin strips, or cut them lengthwise into long thin slices, about ⅛ inch/3 mm thick. Place the vegetable strips in a large bowl.

Pour the hot water into a medium saucepan. Place the pan over high heat, add the salt, and bring the water to a boil.

Pour the boiling water over the carrot and daikon, and let them sit for 3 to 5 minutes. This will soften and slightly cook the vegetables, so they will last longer and absorb the brine better. You don't want them too soft, though; they should still be crunchy when you drain them.

Drain the vegetables and transfer them to another large bowl. Add the pickle brine, and mix well.

Transfer the vegetables and brine to sealed containers or sterilized jars (page 134), making sure the carrot and daikon are fully submerged in the brine. Leave the pickles in the fridge overnight before serving.

To serve, squeeze out any residual brine. The pickles will keep for up to 2 weeks in the fridge.

Note: Daikon radish—also known as mooli—is available in many supermarkets, in oriental shops, or in Indian or Turkish greengrocers.

SAUCES

Dipping Sauce
(*Nuoc Cham*)

In Vietnamese, *Nuoc* means water, and *cham* means to dip, so *nuoc cham* literally means dipping sauce. If we had to pick one dish to epitomize this cookbook, it would have to be nuoc cham. Here is the union of sweet, sour, spicy, bitter, and salty, and the dominance or mildness of any one flavor is dependent on the dish it accompanies.

Nuoc cham is a complex combination of flavors, and if you don't get it right the first time, it's very difficult to distinguish what to adjust, whether to add more sugar, lemon juice, fish sauce, or just water. In Vietnam, nuoc cham is usually prepared in consultation with other family members, and it's a great compliment to your palate to be asked your opinion on the matter. Some people chop the garlic and chiles, while others grind them using a mortar and pestle or press them using the broad side of a knife. We use a food processor to chop them finely and always have a small container stored in the fridge, where they keep for a couple of days. Whichever way you choose, be sure to taste the sauce after adding each ingredient. There are endless variations on nuoc cham. At Banhmi11 we add finely chopped pineapple to give it a sweet note. We also add ginger and dill when we are serving it with fish, and we add tamarind when we are serving it with summer rolls. Some recipes are spicier, some are more sour, some are dark and concentrated like a sauce, and some are light like a dressing.

Garlic, Lime, and Chile Dipping Sauce

**MAKES ABOUT
1 CUP/240 ML**

2 tablespoons granulated sugar
6 tablespoons warm water
4 tablespoons freshly squeezed
  lime juice
2 tablespoons crushed garlic
4 tablespoons fish sauce
1 teaspoon finely chopped
  bird's-eye chile
Freshly ground black pepper

In a medium bowl, dissolve the sugar in the warm water, stirring until there are no visible grains of sugar in the mixture. Once the sugar has completely dissolved, add the lime juice. Taste as you go to ensure that the dressing is to your liking. At this point, it should taste like really good limeade. Add the garlic and stir well. Gradually stir in the fish sauce, adding just enough to suit your taste. (This way you can control the fish sauce's pungency.) Add the chopped chile and then grind over some fresh pepper to taste.

Ginger and Dill Dipping Sauce

**MAKES ABOUT
1 CUP/240 ML**

1 tablespoon granulated sugar
4 tablespoons warm water
1 tablespoon freshly squeezed
  lime juice
1 teaspoon chopped garlic
1 tablespoon fish sauce
2 teaspoons finely chopped fresh
  ginger
2 tablespoons finely chopped
  fresh dill
Finely chopped fresh chiles
Freshly ground black pepper

Dissolve the sugar in the warm water, stirring until there are no visible grains of sugar in the mixture. Once the sugar has completely dissolved, stir in the lime juice. Add the garlic and stir well. Gradually stir in the fish sauce, adding just enough to suit your taste. Add the ginger and stir well. Stir in the chopped dill. Add chopped chile to taste and season the sauce as needed with some black pepper.

Peanut Dipping Sauce

**MAKES ABOUT
1 CUP/240 ML**

1 tablespoon glutinous rice powder

3 tablespoons cold water

1 teaspoon vegetable oil

½ teaspoon crushed garlic

2 cups/200 g crushed roasted,
  salted peanuts

1 teaspoon fish sauce

1 teaspoon salt

1 tablespoon granulated sugar

3 tablespoons hot water

1 tablespoon white wine

In a small bowl, mix the glutinous rice powder with the cold water until the powder dissolves in the water completely.

Heat the oil in a medium heavy-bottomed pan over medium heat; add the garlic and toss until the oil becomes fragrant, being careful not to let the garlic burn. Add the peanuts and toss them in the garlic oil for a couple of minutes until the garlic just starts to brown.

Now pour the rice powder water over the peanuts and stir in a circular motion for a couple of minutes to combine the sauce well.

In a medium bowl, mix together the fish sauce, salt, sugar, and hot water; add this mixture to the peanut sauce and stir well to combine. Cook, stirring constantly, until the sauce is slightly thickened, a couple of minutes or less. Remove the pan from the heat and, using a hand blender or food processor, blend the sauce until it is smooth and uniform in color.

Stir the white wine into the sauce to finish.

Tamarind Sauce

MAKES ABOUT
1 CUP/240 ML

2 tablespoons/20 g tamarind pulp

4 tablespoons warm water

2 tablespoons granulated sugar

2 tablespoons fish sauce

1 teaspoon finely chopped
lemongrass

1 tablespoon crushed garlic

1 tablespoon gia vi (or a mix
of 2 parts sugar, 1 part sea salt,
1 part ground black pepper,
1 part garlic powder)

1 teaspoon cayenne pepper

Tamarind sauce is a versatile sweet and sour sauce, which can be used for cooking or dipping. It works great as a condiment for grilled fish and seafood, adding a fragrant tangy flavor with more depth than citrus; its sweet notes enhance any dish.You can find tamarind in Asian food shops or online. It's frequently used in Indian, Chinese, Thai, and Vietnamese cooking. Use the pulp that comes in plastic-wrapped slabs, not the paste that comes in jars, and cut out a fraction of the slab, as if slicing fudge.

Place the tamarind pulp in a small bowl, add the warm water, and soak for 10 to 20 minutes, until the tamarind pulp becomes soft and dissolves. Strain the juice into a medium bowl.

Stir the sugar into the tamarind juice. Gradually stir in the fish sauce and lemongrass, followed by the garlic, gia vi, and cayenne. Depending on your palate, you may like the sauce slightly more sour or sweet, so adjust as you see fit.

EPILOGUE

When Anh and I first started cooking at our market stall on Broadway Market, we had no idea what path it would lead us down or how much it would change the way we eat and live. Like many in our generation, we were lost in making a living, while never quite feeling like we had a life. We adhered to recipes for success that were cooked up by others, having our plate full but were still famished, until we found the courage to follow our gut. We never trained as chefs but we were young and hungry to taste the world in all its flavors. It's still too early to say whether Bep Collective will succeed; we have done a lot and we are hungry to do more. Our cooking is about hopes and dreams, and finding the ingredients to create them—a purpose, a passion and people who believe— makes living a magnificent feast.

COOKS' NOTES

Basic Ingredients

Eggs Whenever you can, buy free-range or organic eggs. They are more expensive but taste better. Buy them from the farmers' market where they are usually cheaper and fresher.

Gia vi This seasoning mix is especially popular in Northern Vietnamese cooking. It is a combination of garlic salt, sea salt, sugar, and black pepper. The commercial type sold in Asian supermarkets will also contain a small amount of glutamate. To make your own, mix together 2 parts sugar, 1 part sea salt, 1 part freshly ground black pepper, and 1 part garlic powder. Store the gia vi in an airtight jar at room temperature.

Salt Use sea salt unless otherwise specified. Salt is used sparingly in Vietnamese cooking, typically for pickling or cleansing. Fish sauce is a more delicious alternative used to flavor dishes.

Sugar Use granulated sugar unless otherwise specified. Vietnamese cooking uses a variety of sugars, including palm sugar and rock sugar. However, we've found that caster sugar works great as a substitute for those coarser sugars.

Black pepper Vietnam remains one of the main producers of black pepper. Most is produced in the Central Highlands region, where the red basalt earth is ideal for growing it. The best black pepper is said to come from the island of Phu Quoc. Use whole black peppercorns and grind them as you go to retain their intense flavor.

Vietnamese Pantry

Fresh Spices

Onions

We use smaller red onions, as we find that they have more flavor and are easier to handle than large white onions.

Shallots

We are not fussy about using Thai or imported shallots from Asian countries. These usually have a deep red color and a strong taste, but they are small and difficult to peel. Our favorites are banana shallots, usually of French origin. The round yellow shallots also work well.

Garlic

The easiest way to peel a garlic clove is to smash it first using a mortar and pestle or the broad side of a knife, and then peel off the skin. We crush garlic in a food processor and then keep a small jar in the fridge for that week's cooking. Alternatively, you can chop the cloves as you go.

Ginger

Fresh ginger (ginger root) works well in broths and seafood dishes. English organic ginger is usually quite small. The most common fresh ginger is the large rhizome from China, and you can find it in the produce aisle of most supermarkets.

Galangal

Galangal looks similar to ginger, but its skin is smoother and it doesn't have ginger's lemony taste. We use galangal with fish and meat to make them fragrant. It's best to grind galangal using a mortar and pestle or a food processor. We buy it frozen from Asian supermarkets, thaw it in hot water, and use it as fresh.

Lemongrass

Lemongrass is one of the most versatile ingredients, and lends its aroma to any soup or grilled dish. We use both the whole fresh lemongrass stalks as well as chopped lemongrass, which you can find frozen in Asian supermarkets. Lemongrass can also be used to make tea.

Tamarind	The whole ripe fruit looks a bit like a broad bean, and is brown in color. You can eat ripe tamarind, through it is typically it's used to add sourness to a dish. Tamarind is wonderful as it has a mild sourness and very fruity notes. Usually it's sold as a block of pulp in Asian supermarkets. We break a bit off from the block, then pour boiling hot water over it to dilute it and make tamarind juice (page 221). Note: if you can't find tamarind, use lemon or lime juice.
Chiles	For a real spicy kick, we use Scotch bonnets, green chiles from Kenya, or red chiles from Thailand. They keep for months in the freezer; we just take a couple out at a time, wash them under the tap, and use them as needed.
Mushrooms	There are two types of mushrooms that are primarily used in Vietnamese cooking: shiitake and wood ear mushrooms. Shiitakes, available fresh or dried, add flavor to meat and stocks. Wood ear mushrooms, available only in dried form, are usually mixed with meat to add crunch. We take a handful of dried mushrooms, soak them in hot water, and they expand significantly as they rehydrate. Wash the mushrooms carefully under running water before using, as they may contain grains of sand. Squeeze out the water before slicing them.
Kaffir lime leaves	These usually come frozen, and you can find them in Asian supermarkets. Wash a few leaves to thaw them and use a pair of scissors to cut them into thin strips. Sprinkle them over chicken or white fish.

Fresh Herbs

Fresh herbs are one of the most prominent characteristics of Vietnamese cooking. Rarely is a meal served without a plateful of fresh herbs. Here we have listed the most popular and readily available herbs. To make your own herb plate, mix a few salad greens, torn lettuce leaves, a couple of slices of cucumber, and a mixture of fresh herbs.

Many of these herbs can be found in large supermarkets, and Asian supermarkets have regular imports of the herbs into the UK. We find that Turkish greengrocers offer the best value, stocking cilantro, dill, and mint throughout the year, generally in bigger bunches than you find in regular supermarkets.

Cilantro	Cilantro is perhaps the most versatile of herbs. We use the whole sprigs for garnishing just about any dish, and mix the chopped leaves with spring onion to use in soups. The large bunches look deceptively similar to parsley, but the taste is very different. Choose young cilantro, which is smaller and leafier than older plants, and lacks the hard stems, which we don't use anyway.
Mint	Spearmint, as you find it in greengrocers and supermarkets, is delicious and keeps for a week or so in water. Use the leaves only.
Basil	Thai basil, as it is usually called, is different from Italian basil, so don't use the latter as a substitute. Thai basil has green, pointy leaves and a quite unique aroma, reminiscent of cinnamon and cloves. It goes especially well with beef dishes.
Hot mint	This herb is not easy to find, but it's very rewarding when you do. Asian supermarkets often stock it. Herb growers in the UK and elsewhere also plant it, so you can sometimes find it in farmers' markets. Rau ram has a peppery taste that goes really well with meat and seafood. Note: if you can't find rau ram, the closest substitute is cilantro.
Shiso	You may have seen this herb on sushi plates, but most people tend to discard it. The Vietnamese variety has both a deep purplish red side and a green side. Shiso is said to have great healing qualities, and one Vietnamese remedy for colds is a chicken rice soup with plenty of chopped *tia to* and spring onion.

Dry Goods

Rice

In Vietnamese markets, you will find basketfuls of various types of rice, all freshly harvested. The Vietnamese typically use good-quality, long-grain jasmine rice. Personally, we prefer short-grain rice such as Korean arirang rice or sushi rice because it has the right degree of "stickiness." We don't use risotto rice, parboiled rice, or basmati rice in Vietnamese dishes. Sometimes blending different types of rice can also work well. To cook rice you usually need 2 parts water to 1 part rice.

Rice paper

In Vietnam, rice paper is often made from a mixture of rice flour and water, which is formed into thin sheets, like crepes, and then sundried on large bamboo racks. The rice paper for export is usually factory-made and tends to be thicker, which makes it easier to handle, especially when making summer rolls. The most popular type is plain white with a diameter of 7 to 8½ inches/18 to 22 cm. We recommend dabbing rice papers with warm water and then letting them rest on a wet cloth when preparing your rolls (pages 185). This way, the papers are less likely to stick to each other or tear.

Rice vermicelli noodles (Bun)

These are round, long noodles, a bit like spaghetti, but made with rice flour. They can be quite thick, about ½ inch/1.2 cm in diameter, making them suitable for noodle soups (such as bun bo Hue), or they can be quite thin, ¼ inch/0.6 cm in diameter, making them suitable for noodle salads. In Vietnam they are made fresh daily. But you can also get very good dried bun noodles.

Flat rice noodles (Pho)

These flat noodles are used exclusively in pho dishes, either in noodle soups or in stir-fries. They are quite similar to the Chinese *ho fun* noodles, although the Vietnamese version is thinner and has more elasticity. You can get fresh *ho fun* noodles from Chinese supermarkets, or you can use the dehydrated type and rehydrate them in the same way as you would rice vermicelli noodles.

Cellophane or glass noodles (Mien)

These are very thin transparent noodles, made from mung beans or arrowroot. They can be quite brittle when dry and require gentle handling. As they get soft very quickly, they only need soaking in hot water before using, as in spring rolls for instance. You can use glass noodles or rice vermicelli in many noodle soup recipes, so work with whatever you have on hand. As a general rule, glass noodles have their own flavor characteristics, whereas rice vermicelli noodles are neutral in flavor. For instance, for a clear broth like chicken, glass noodles work well. But for bold flavors, like the spicy *bun bo Hue*, or sweet and sour noodle soups, rice vermicelli noodles make a better starch base.

Dried shallots

Dried shallots are used liberally in Vietnamese salads, stir-fries, and noodle soups. You can buy them in jars from Asian supermarkets, or you can buy dried onion from any supermarket and lightly toast it. Alternatively, to make your own dried shallots, remove the skin from the shallots and then slice them into very thin rings; dehydrate the shallot rings by placing them on a baking sheet in a cool oven (200°F/100°C/gas 4) for an hour. Then fry them in hot oil in a frying pan until slightly brown, taking care not to bum them. Remove with a slotted spoon to a plate lined with a paper towel and let them rest. You can then use them immediately or store them in the fridge in an airtight container for 2 to 3 weeks. If they turn soft in the fridge, revive them by placing them in the oven at 350°F/180°C/gas 4 for a couple of minutes.

Roasted peanuts

Buy salted roasted peanuts and crush them coarsely in a food processor. Use to sprinkle on salads and vegetables or to make Peanut Dipping Sauce (page 220).

Fermented Products

Fish sauce

Fish sauce is the holy grail of Vietnamese cuisine, and a good teaspoonful covers a multitude of sins. Traditionally, it's made using only two ingredients: anchovies and salt. The fish are fermented in sea salt and kept in large wooden barrels in the shade for a year, after which time the dear, golden liquid is extracted and bottled. The protein content of fish sauce is usually a good indicator of its quality, with the gourmet types containing up to 4 g of protein per tablespoon.

Shrimp paste

Fermented shrimp paste has a very pungent smell. However, diluting the shrimp paste (see page 231) to use as a seasoning for broths, or combining it with garlic, lime juice, and chile, eliminates the pungent smell, leaving just the wonderful flavors.

Techniques

Meat carpaccio

Wrap the meat in plastic wrap and place it in the freezer for a couple of hours. The meat should be partly frozen, but not solid, when it comes out of the freezer. Use a sharp knife to cut thin slices of meat.

Fish carpaccio

For fish like sea bass, wrap the fillets in plastic wrap and put them in the freezer for 30 minutes before slicing thinly. Alternatively, cut thick slices of fish, wrap the individual slices in butcher's paper, and freeze the packages for 20 minutes; then use a rolling pin to pound the fish until it flattens.

Making diluted shrimp paste

Pour cold water into a bowl, add the shrimp paste, and stir well so that the shrimp paste completely dissolves. Let this liquid rest for around 20 minutes. The liquid will stay at the top and the sediment will sink to the bottom. Pour off the liquid into a separate bowl and discard the rest.

Cooking dried noodles

Noodles for the Vietnamese are like pasta for the Italians: they come in all shapes and sizes. Dried noodles taste as good as fresh ones if you use the correct technique. Remove the noodles from their packaging and put them in a large bowl of cool water. Leave them to soak for 20 minutes. In a pan, bring to a boil enough water to cover the noodles and pour in a little oil to prevent them from sticking. Add the drained noodles to the boiling water; turn down the heat and gently stir them. Cook until the noodles are al dente (7 to 8 minutes for 14 ounces/400 g). Once the noodles are tender, drain them, rinse them under cool running water, and untangle them with a fork before serving.

SOURCES

Markets

Our first port of call for fresh, seasonal ingredients is always the farmers' market. In most large cities, there is at least one, with gorgeous local produce. Look out for when your local farmers' market is held.

We love the meat, fish, and vegetables from our fellow stall holders in London, and in markets all over the world you can find growers and farmers who are truly passionate about good food and who will pitch up in rain or shine. We probably do spend more at the markets than we could have at supermarkets, but the ingredients are better than restaurant-quality, and with simple cooking, it's a beautiful way to eat high-quality food without the four-star restaurant prices.

Specialists

Ingredients such as fresh herbs, fish sauce, and rice paper are now widely available in most supermarkets. We supplement by visiting the smaller Asian, Turkish, Indian, Bangladeshi, and Jamaican grocers nearby for spices and ethnic produce, such as daikon (mooli) or tamarind. Most cities have a Chinatown, or an international grocery where you can find the more exotic products called for in this cookbook. Finally, I want to reiterate that Vietnamese cooking—and our ethos in general—is all about versatility. So if you don't have access to authentic ingredients, then use your imagination and improvise!

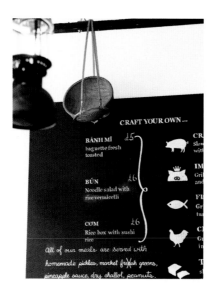

CRAFT YOUR OWN ...

BÁNH MÌ £5
baguette fresh
toasted

BÚN £6
Noodle salad with
rice vermicelli

CƠM £6
Rice box with sushi
rice

*All of our meals are served with
homemade pickles, market fresh greens,
pineapple sauce, dry shallot, peanuts.*

phát triển
đồng cỏ
chăn nuôi

ACKNOWLEDGMENTS

Love and gratitude to all our colleagues and friends at Bep Collective, present and previous. Thank you for believing in us and coming on board. You are and always will be our Banhmily.

Thanks to Simon Kaempfer, Yuki Suguira, Valerie Berry, Lirong and Patrick, and Risa and Yasu, for our creative education and helping us to realize our aesthetic vision.

Thanks to Broadway Market fellow traders for teaching us about provenance, passion for pursuing one's own journey and community. Thank you, Andy Veitch, for giving us the chance to get started!

Thanks to our families—we never see you enough, and we never say it in words, but we care. We owe you everything for who we are today.

Thanks to our friends for keeping us sane.

To our UK editor, Rowan Yapp, and Rosemary Davidson, thank you for your guidance and endless support. To our U.S. editor, Kristen Green Wiewora, thank you for making the book even more beautiful.

Above all, thank you to everyone who has chosen to eat with us. You taught us everything we know now and your support is the reason we are still here today. This is our chance to be the generation that takes food back to basics—natural, beautiful, and bountiful.

ABOUT THE AUTHORS

Van Tran and Anh Vu represent a new generation of foodies and entrepreneurs, changing expectations of fresh, urban, egalitarian food experiences.

Born in Hanoi eleven months part, they both spent their childhoods in Vietnam, immersed in the country's rich culinary traditions. Van and Anh received scholarships to come to the U.S. and UK to study before meeting at Oxford University. They didn't train professionally as chefs but worked in finance in New York and London before leaving the city to pursue their passion.

They started their market stall sensation, Banhmi11, at Broadway Market in 2009 and went on to found Bep Collective, opening 101 Great Eastern St, Shoreditch in 2012, 17 Elm Street, Chancery Lane in 2013 and 40 Bow Lane, St Paul in 2014.

Van and Anh were named Young British Foodies by the *Guardian* and have made television appearances with Nigel Slater and Jamie Oliver. Their recipes are regularly featured in the *Telegraph*, the *Guardian* and *Waitrose Magazine*, among other international publications. Banhmi11 has been listed in Time Out's "100 Top Dishes in London," and in *ShortList* magazine's "The World's 10 Best Sandwiches." They live in East London.

Please visit them at www.bepcollective.com.

INDEX

Note: Page references in *italics* indicate photographs.